FOREWORD BY JOE PULIZZI
THE GODFATHER OF CONTENT MARKETING

BRIAN PIPER

EPIC

CONTENT

MARKETING

FOR HIGHER EDUCATION

HOW TO CONNECT WITH STUDENTS, ALUMNI, FACULTY, STAFF, AND OTHERS TO BUILD TRUST **AND REACH YOUR INSTITUTIONAL GOALS**

Epic Content Marketing
For Higher Education

Brian Piper

ISBN: 979-8-9898626-3-4 (Paperback)

T̄ TILT
PUBLISHING

700 Park Offices Drive, Suite 250
Research Triangle, NC 27709

To my wife, Jenn, and my mother, Kathryn, thank you both for inspiring me and motivating me every day.

Contents

Foreword

As far as I can tell, animals cannot tell stories. I've never heard a horse share an intimate tale with another horse. I've never seen a mouse whisper about harrowing adventures to other mice. It just doesn't happen.

No, storytelling is exclusively a human superpower.

For thousands of years, humans have been sharing stories with other humans to educate, entertain, and inspire. Stories help shape our beliefs. They give us meaning. They give humans a reason to exist and grow. We find purpose through stories.

They are also our fuel for modern marketing.

I've been helping organizations create, tell, and share their stories for over two decades. I've been blessed to work directly with amazing brands like Disney, HP, Microsoft, Autodesk and LEGO. Boy, do they have stories to tell.

But, believe it or not, of all the business-to-business and business-to-consumer brands out there, higher education institutions have the most stories to tell.

The students. The alumni. The faculty and staff.

Inside the classroom. At the recital. Around the quad.

There are stories everywhere. There are stories about how that one student did that great thing against all odds. Stories about how an alumni broke through multiple barriers, shaped by what the University provided. Story after story after story.

Stories that, if captured and disseminated correctly, would surely attract more students. It would most definitely increase alumni donations. It would make the current student population, and their parents, feel that much better about their college choice.

Stories told in print. In email. On podcasts. Via video.

What an amazing blessing for an institution to have so many stories to tell.

Alas, most higher education institutions are, to be frank, terrible at finding, telling, and promoting their stories. Whether this is a general taboo that higher ed has against marketing, or a sheer lack of strategy and processes, the majority of universities are failing at content marketing.

Strike that. They aren't failing. Most don't even have a documented content marketing strategy.

Whether that is your current position, or whether you are a dabbler and want to get serious about developing Epic Content Marketing for your institution, this book is for you. The author of this book, my colleague and friend for almost a decade, is uniquely positioned to guide you through this journey.

Look around you. Look at all the stories that can and should be told… to educate, entertain, and inspire. Finding and sharing these stories is not just good business, it's your obligation as a higher ed marketer.

You have been designated as the storyteller for your organization. Now is the time to use this superpower wisely.

Yours in Content,
Joe Pulizzi
Bestselling author of nine books, including Epic Content Marketing. Founder, Tilt Publishing.

Acknowledgments

There are too many people for me to thank without starting an entirely separate book just for that. Every one of the people I interviewed provided valuable insights and kept me motivated and moving forward.

I wanted to create a chapter where I could thank each one individually and talk about how they inspire me in my work, but this would be a much longer book. So as you read each quote, check these people out on LinkedIn, connect with them, and consume their content. You will not be disappointed.

Writing a book is not an easy process, and I have to thank the prolific writers and creators I know who show me that you can consistently create valuable and engaging content that makes a difference.

Jay Acunzo and Melanie Deziel kept me focused and driven with their advice in their Creator Kitchen community.

Mark Schaefer and his RISE community provided endless thought starters and a sounding board.

Robert Rose launched his book, Content Marketing Strategy, during my writing process, and I read it whenever I wasn't writing. It was the perfect complement to my process.

Ann Handley put out her Total Annarchy newsletter every two weeks. It was invariably delivered when I was sitting at my desk trying to put together the next thought or organizing the latest round of quotes, and her writing reminded me why it was all worth it—and it made me laugh, as always.

And, of course, Joe Pulizzi who started it all when he offered me the opportunity to co-author the second edition of Epic Content Marketing with him back on October 13, 2021. Recently, he launched Tilt Publishing, which is taking these words and turning them into an actual book. I have talked to other people who have self-published, and it sounded like a difficult process. The amazing team at Tilt Publishing has made this so easy. They are over there editing, setting, designing, and all the other things I am not even aware of to make this happen.

A final thanks to my kids (all of them), my mother and father, and my wife, Jenn. Without her, this would not be possible as I would have stopped writing long ago, or I would still be writing with no end in sight. She is my soulmate and my rock. She is also my first-line editor who saves me from myself more times than I can count.

Introduction

Why do we need another book on content marketing? Aren't there already two editions of Epic Content Marketing and scores of other books focused on it? Do we really need a book specifically for higher education content marketing?

Apparently, yes, we do. While doing the research for this book, I spoke to more than 50 higher education leaders and marketers, as well as numerous B2B (business-to-business) and B2C (business-to-consumer) marketers. Other than a handful of institutions (the ones I used as case studies), every person I interviewed struggled to come up with examples of higher education institutions that were doing effective content marketing—or any content marketing, for that matter.

Content marketing is an ideal strategy for higher education because we have so many stories available. Whether from our students, faculty, staff, or alumni, we have a wealth of inspiring content options that can connect with many of our audiences.

Our entire goal, as institutions, is to provide value, learning, and experience; to build a relationship of trust with a network of resources, while providing career and lifelong learning opportunities to our audiences, including students, alumni, faculty, and staff. And that is exactly what content marketing is all about.

So why do we not see more examples of epic content marketing in higher education?

Teresa Flannery is the executive vice president and chief operating officer for CASE (Council for Advancement and Support of Education). In Terry's book, How to Market a University, she talks about the fact that marketing itself has been almost taboo in higher education up until the past five to ten years.

According to Flannery, "College and university leaders have been slow to recognize that strategic integrated marketing is beneficial for meeting all of these goals, but in recent years marketing has come of age in higher education." [1]

I cannot recommend her book enough, and I keep a heavily Post-it-noted copy of it on the right side of my desk.

"I'd say there's constant talk about marketing, [but] there is little agreement about what marketing is. In many cases, particularly at highly selective institutions, there is little appetite for creating the resources that would be necessary to do sustained marketing. And there's not a very strong internal political constituency for it, unless it directly affects your program or department."

> — Michael Schoenfeld, partner, global co-lead for foundations, education, and global health sector, Brunswick Group.
> Michael spent more than 25 years in higher education as the chief communications officer at Duke and Vanderbilt Universities.

Book Whisperers

In Terry's book, she describes her writing process, which is based on an idea from Professor James Thurber. She reached out to colleagues and experts she knew in different areas of higher education marketing and had conversations with them that helped her create and craft the different sections of her book.

I thought this was a brilliant methodology and decided to try it as well. It worked great. Not only did I get to talk with incredibly smart people who were experts in their particular areas, but I got to connect with a whole new group of higher education thought leaders whom I probably would not have met otherwise.

Book Collaborators

You will find quotes from a variety of experts scattered throughout the book, insights and opinions I was excited to uncover while having those conversations. I felt that adding this knowledge from a community of experts was going to provide more value than what I would deliver on my own.

I started doing these interviews the same way Terry did, but after finding so many nuggets of wisdom, I decided to pass them on verbatim.

My journey with this book started as an exploration into applying what I learned while writing the second edition of Epic Content Marketing to higher education. It finished with a massive collaboration of knowledge and insights from many of the people I respect and admire in both marketing and higher education.

How to Read This Book

There are as many unique ways to read this book as there are different types of people. Well, maybe not that many; it is just a book. But there are takeaways for everyone. If you have not done much (or any) content marketing, by all means: read the entire thing. If you want a deep dive into all the particulars of content marketing in general, read the second edition of Epic Content Marketing that I co-authored with Joe Pulizzi. The first few chapters of this book start broad and focus on content marketing fundamentals relevant to higher education, but I dive deeper into the specifics as the book progresses.

You can also pick and choose the sections that are most applicable to you. I would recommend that everyone who picks up this book read the case studies, the chapters on content optimization and discovery, and the chapter on the future of content marketing in higher education.

I have tried to keep the content interesting and educational. I am a huge fan of Ann Handley, an amazing marketer, speaker, and writer. I keep the latest edition of her book, Everybody Writes, on the left side of my desk (opposite Terry's book), and refer to it regularly to help me keep myself and my writing fresh and focused.

In one of Ann's recent newsletters, she talked about the importance of remembering your audience while you write and constantly asking, "So what," which I have attempted to do at every step of this writing and editing process.

Also, as much as I enjoy leveraging AI while I work and create, I stayed away from it during the actual writing process. I did reach out to Perplexity for some research, ChatGPT and Claude to help with some outline ideas (mostly checking what I had already created to see what I was missing), and I use Grammarly extensively for editing (although I occasionally disagree with it and do not listen to its recommendations), but this book is human-written and edited.

EPIC RESOURCES

1. Teresa M. Flannery, *How to Market a University: Building Value in a Competitive Environment* (Johns Hopkins University Press, 2021), 2.

CHAPTER 1

What Is Content Marketing?

There are lots of books and resources that dive deep into what content marketing is, but, at the highest level, it is using content in a way that helps solve a problem or answer a question for your target audience.

In the second edition of *Epic Content Marketing*, we define content marketing this way: "Content marketing is the marketing and business process for creating and distributing valuable and compelling content to attract, acquire, and engage a clearly defined and understood target audience—with the objective of driving profitable customer action." [1]

What turns your standard content into content marketing comes down to those three things: "valuable and compelling content," "clearly defined and understood target audience," and "driving profitable customer action."

Now, your profitable customer action may be way down the road. It might take dozens of pieces of content—videos, social posts, podcasts, news stories, etc.—before your particular audience takes any profitable action. Still, you are always driving them toward taking action, even if that is only to read more of your content, sign up for your newsletter, or share a post with their network.

One of the most difficult things to explain to leadership is that your target audience may never take any action due to your content marketing, and that is all right.

"Content marketing is a way to be discovered that also provides value."

> — Dayana Kibilds, strategist, Ologie, speaker, co-author of *Mailed It: A Guide to Crafting Emails That Build Relationships and Get Results,* host of Enrollify's *Talking Tactics* podcast

With the incredible amount of content that is produced in higher education and the frenetic pace that often accompanies that content creation, it is easy for teams to lose focus on the "valuable" and "targeted audience" parts. And if the creators and editors are not specifically tasked with marketing, they will certainly not focus on the "call to action" part.

Many of the content creator roles in higher education marketing departments today came from more traditional PR or communications departments, and they may not have been creating content to drive action or other marketing-based goals.

"Content marketing is critically important, but is still in its infancy in higher ed. I think we're just scratching the surface in this work, but, in many ways, we've been doing it around the edges, and unintentionally. The organizational shifts that we've seen over the last 10 to 15 years with the traditional communications newsroom side of the house and the marketing side of the house coming together, becoming integrated marketing communications teams, is what is turbocharging this. You're starting to see that cross-pollination between the content side and the marketing side."

> — Angela Polec, vice president for strategic marketing and communications, Temple University

While in many ways we are just getting started with content marketing in higher education, there is no doubt that it has incredible potential across numerous audiences and initiatives. The institutions that are already using it are seeing excellent results.

"We have found, through our data, the touchpoint of content marketing is as valuable as a visit to campus."

> — Allison Turcio, assistant vice president for enrollment and marketing,
> Siena College, host of Enrollify's *The Application* podcast

Even beyond creating measurable value for the institution, content marketing creates value for the audience. Content is the way that audiences come to know, like, and trust your institution. Content connects with audiences in a way that traditional ads struggle to do. This consistent and valuable content is the foundation of a relationship that you are trying to form with your ideal user.

"Content marketing is incredibly important as part of a strategy. There's certainly sales content, but there is also this idea of being that trusted voice. Part of our obligation is to be that voice and provide content focused on what you need to know to go to college. Our hope is that we're that trusted voice, and they choose us, but the reality is, we want to be providing that information for anybody."

> — Carrie Phillips, chief communications and marketing officer,
> University of Arkansas at Little Rock

"Content marketing is very important in this day and age, when a university can't rely on traditional media to help get its story out. It is up to us to do the storytelling and to connect with our audiences. Our job is to tell our story to the largest number of people possible in the best way possible. And that's increasingly by doing content marketing. It's going to be even more and more crucial going forward."

> — Dave Tyler, director of university social media,
> Rochester Institute of Technology

Content marketing works very well for B2B and B2C businesses, and there are many examples and case studies across sectors. Content marketing can get messy in higher education because there are a lot of different audiences that we create content for and we are not always trying to directly drive profitable customer action with all those audiences.

For example, when we create content for alumni, we are not always just trying to get them to donate money. Sometimes, we are trying to build connections or create a sense of belonging in those groups. Or we are just trying to increase the pride they have in the institution.

While that content may not drive direct profit, it does create more value for the institution by improving the reputation within that audience, creating a strong network, and expanding the opportunities for the people within it.

"Content marketing is critical, non-optional, and essentially required for the present and future success of higher ed, for a couple of reasons. Content marketing is either the way that a potential student, staff member, parent, or other important audience finds out about the school, or it's the way their opinions of that school are ratified. Both of those are massively important in answering, 'How do we get students? How do we get staff? How do we get the things that we want?'"

— Jay Baer, business growth and customer experience researcher,
author, advisor, speaker

Higher education institutions create content for a lot of channels, and content is being created by different teams across the institution. In many cases, that content is created without a lot of connection or collaboration between those teams or the individuals creating it. In the higher education community, there are always conversations about the silos we face and the impact they have on our work.

One of the biggest problems with these silos when it comes to content marketing is that all the content coming from many places across the institution can sound different, have different messages, communicate different values, and reach different goals.

It is hard enough to differentiate your institution within the higher education category, and it is even more difficult if your audiences see inconsistent messages and statements coming from several departments or schools within a single institution. In this environment, where there are so many choices, it is more critical than ever to have unified messaging and be a singularly branded house instead of a house of brands.

"Content marketing is critically important because there are so many institutions, and if you look at our actual mission statements, they're all so similar. Content marketing allows institutions to talk about what they do well in ways that are specifically focused on the interests of their audiences."

> — Teresa Valerio Parrot, EdD, APR, principal, TVP Communications, co-host of *Trusted Voices* podcast

One of the reasons that we in higher education are uniquely positioned to excel at content marketing is because of the vast number of stories we have at our disposal. We are already in the business of sharing knowledge and informing audiences. We have deep wells of expertise to draw from, and we tend to have a lot of original research, which is some of the highest-performing content in the digital landscape.

One of the biggest problems we face, however, due to having so many stories and potential content, is deciding what really matters and what will make a difference or help us reach our goals.

Requested Content

Whether the request is from a dean, a senior leader, or a researcher, there are a lot of people putting in requests for content they think we should create. Typically, these stories deliver information the requester deems important but that may not align with what the audience is looking for.

We started tagging the news stories we created at the University of Rochester to be able to track performance on the stories that our content officers and editors came up with, versus the stories that were brought to us by researchers, deans, and faculty. After three years of compiling the data on more than 500 stories, we decided that we had enough results to report the findings. While there was incredible content and high-performing stories on both sides, the stories that our marketing communications (marcom) staff created had three times as much total traffic and five times as much organic traffic compared to the stories that were brought to us.

I am not saying the stories that were brought to us did not need to be told or did not deserve the attention they received, but the data shows that carefully selecting content, based on trending topics in society, leads to more engagement and visibility than simply distributing content because someone finds that content important to them or their goals.

Too Much Content

As higher education institutions, we create a *lot* of content. That was one of the first things I noticed when I was doing research for my job interview at the University of Rochester. *So. Much. Content!*

While having numerous audiences to connect and communicate with can be a challenge for higher education marketers, it can also be a huge benefit when it comes to finding sources of content. Every one of our students, faculty, staff, and alumni have stories to tell. There is no shortage of content. But that is also a double-edged sword.

"The problem is having too much content and not having the discipline and the tools to say 'no, this is our roadmap, and we're going to stick with it.' People are flooded with so much content these days; you have to pick and choose and curate."

— Bill Faust, president, Ologie

"When you tell every story, you are actually telling no story. One of the things that higher ed really struggles with is trying to talk about every department. All it does is confuse the message. You've got to lean into a differentiator. You have to play the 'only we' game, like: only we can do this thing. If you don't really know what that [thing] is, that's probably a challenge. Leaning into what truly makes you different is sorely needed in most places."

— Jay Baer, business growth and customer experience researcher,
author, advisor, speaker

A high-level content marketing strategy can change all of that. A content marketing strategy can provide the focal point for all content creators across the institution. More about that in the next chapter.

"Content marketing really is a privilege. The idea that we can just pick up our phones and instantly publish something to one of the hundreds of free platforms on the Internet and have our ideas be heard is pretty incredible. No longer do we need to rent space in a newspaper or on a billboard or an expensive TV commercial, or print and mail brochures, in order for our value to resonate. There are very few barriers to entry anymore. For higher education institutions to not take part in that privilege would be foolish. Add to that the fact that college is no longer a given for a lot of high school graduates, if we're not putting our stake in the ground online and being a trusted source of thought leadership and influence, people aren't just going to magically appear in seats in classrooms."

— John Azoni, owner and executive producer, Unveild,
host of *Higher Ed Storytelling University* podcast

"Content marketing is important for higher ed because of the way our audiences find information now. They swim around the web, and we [need] to feed the machines. Each individual piece of content is important because anything could be a prospective student's first contact with your institution. And you don't know what it's going to be. Will this take them to the next step? Will this cause them to follow the account to see more, to visit a website, to follow the link you're suggesting, to do the action that you are calling them to do? So keep that in mind: each piece of content means you are successfully marketing, no matter what."

— Andrew Cassel, director of communications and science engagement,
Hubbard Brook Research Foundation

"Content marketing is one of the ways we educate our target audiences about what we have to offer. Advertising is not enough because ads are becoming less trusted by people; they just glance over them. They know it's a sales pitch or an ad. Content marketing, if done right, is a more trusted source of information. It has to be done on an ongoing basis because one piece of information is not enough to get people to believe that education is important. It is an ongoing initiative. Generating content that resonates with your target audiences in an interesting, informative, educational way, and distributing it to the right channels, where they can actually see it, is one of the most important vehicles for us."

— Maya Demishkevich, chief marketing officer,
Carroll Community College

"Content marketing is essential to higher ed, and it's the only type of marketing higher ed should be doing. Higher ed is so well positioned for content marketing. You've got an abundance of collateral, you've got an abundance of material, and there are so many stories to tell. Even if you're saying, 'but we're just a small undergraduate-only school,' trust me, you have more stories than you can tell in a year. You just have to look for them and, to be effective, you have to be good at packaging them."

— Tony Sheridan, senior digital campaigns manager,
KAUST (King Abdullah University of Science and Technology)

EPIC THOUGHTS

- Content marketing involves creating valuable, compelling content targeted to a clearly defined audience with the ultimate goal of driving profitable action, even if that action is delayed.

- Content marketing is still in its early stages in higher education, but it has great potential. Some schools are already seeing content marketing touchpoints being as valuable as campus visits in influencing enrollment.

- Higher education is well-positioned to excel at content marketing given the multitude of stories, expertise, and original research available to draw from. The challenge is deciding what content matters most and aligns with audience interests and institutional goals.

EPIC RESOURCES

1. Joe Pulizzi and Brian Piper, *Epic Content Marketing*, 2nd ed. (McGraw Hill, 2023), 3.

CHAPTER 2

What Is Content Marketing Strategy?

Robert Rose wrote the book on content marketing strategy, literally. It is titled *Content Marketing Strategy*, and it is excellent. If you want a very deep dive into the underbelly of content marketing strategy, I highly recommend it.

"The biggest focus needs to be coordination of content and coordination of story. There needs to be an actual process and strategy for messaging. That coordination is the first and most important step in any institution, and it's probably the most difficult."

— Robert Rose, chief strategy officer, The Content Advisory,
chief strategy advisor, Content Marketing Institute, author,
co-host of *This Old Marketing* podcast

A good strategy is the key to being effective. It is the key to staying on track and staying aligned. Many higher education institutions have (or should have) an institutional strategic plan. It is a roadmap of what matters most to the institution, and it drives your marketing, curriculum, recruiting, and your messaging. Everything should focus on the success of that strategic plan.

That institutional plan should also feed your marketing plan. Whether you are in a single department, a school within the institution, or in central marketing and communications, you need to ensure that your marketing plan, goals, and school initiatives all connect to that larger institutional plan.

Following that same pattern, your strategic content marketing plan should ladder up to your marketing plan *and* your institutional plan (as well as your department/school plan).

Every tactic that you employ, every piece of content you create, and every opportunity to connect with supporters and alumni (or any audience) ought to be intentional and connected to those plans.

Your strategies are your guides to everything.

"In higher education, we assume that things are obvious to our audiences. Every school wants to talk about a comprehensive number of majors with a little plus sign after it. There's this lack of specificity in the product. We're not really clear on what we're selling or marketing to our students. So content marketing is harder because if you're not trying to make a direct connection to sales, you're at least trying to obscure it to some degree where it's palatable to the audience. But if you have no purpose, no idea what you're trying to accomplish, you can't do that effectively—it just becomes random acts of content. And that's not really productive either. Until we can get to that point where we're marketing more specifically and with more resonance for our audiences, it's not going to go anywhere. We're just going to be producing a bunch of stuff crowding the market and competing with AI-generated content because it's all generic and based on the same body of knowledge that is detached from creativity, innovation, and human input. There's a real opportunity to think more specifically, stop trying to be everything to everyone, tighten up what we're doing, and figure out what problems we're actually solving for people. We all grew up with student search being a great way to reach prospects. We buy names, and then just spam, and there's a loyalty to that which continues to shape higher ed marketing. It's reflected in the media too, right? You have press release farms that measure their efficacy based on 300 releases issued, to what end? Did your enrollment go up? Did you see any influx in the areas that you were focused on? Or is it just an arbitrary number, that means nothing for your local regional publications?"

> — Tim Jones, director, brand and integrated strategy,
> SimpsonScarborough

Your strategies form the foundation for all your tracking and measurement. Whether you are using KPIs (key performance indicators) or OKRs (objectives and key results), or both; SMART (specific, measurable, attainable, relevant, and time-based) or PACT (purposeful, actionable, continuous, and trackable) goals; or a red line on a big thermometer poster in your office, your content marketing strategy reveals if your tactics are helping you reach your goals.

One of the complaints I often hear is that you cannot measure the impact of content marketing. There is no direct line to see if a piece of content (or several) resulted in a campus tour request, an application, or a donation. This is not entirely true. More on that in Chapter 13, "Tracking and Optimizing." The more well-defined your content marketing strategy is, the more pointed your tactics will be and your KPIs and OKRs will be clearer. This allows you to more precisely establish baselines, and measure improvement and completion of goals.

"Content marketing is important and not being done effectively for the most part. It's a different way of reaching your audiences. A full-on content marketing strategy could be a game changer for higher ed, and I don't think a lot of folks are doing it."

> — Jaime Hunt, chief marketing officer, Old Dominion University,
> host of *Confessions of a Higher Ed CMO* podcast

So why do most higher education institutions not have content marketing strategies? Why does content typically become an order-taking soup of mixed messages, canned stories, and packaged media?

There are several reasons we hear most often:

Lack of resources: not enough time, personnel, or budget to do what we need to do.

Culture: this is the way we have always done it.

Leadership: we just cannot get buy-in to commit to changing our marketing.

However, I think it generally comes down to one thing: fear. Fear of change. Fear of the unknown. Fear of failure. Fear of trying something new and looking like you do not know what you are doing. From faculty to staff to leadership, so much of the culture in higher education is the belief that we are the experts and know the best way to do things. It seems that, instead, we should adopt a culture of continual learning and experimentation—exactly what we ask of our students.

A good content marketing strategy is designed to be flexible and adjust as the needs and focus of the audiences evolve. It is important to have a plan for what content goes where within your user journey to move your audiences to the next stage, but it is more important to be able to recognize when there is content that is not working, or where there is a gap in content, and to be able to adjust.

You absolutely need all those other things. You need resources, you need to be able to change how you work, and you need support from leadership. But the most important thing you need is the courage and conviction to commit to content marketing -- to give it the time that it needs to work, and to have the confidence that it will overdeliver in helping you reach your goals, even if you do not have systems set up to track all the connections.

"The overarching goal at a university is to create a consistency of voice at a brand level, and that is exactly the opposite of what they tend to do. Universities want to have a completely diverse voice. In order to succeed, they have to have an institutional voice and a brand voice. The institution has to believe in things, otherwise, you get into a situation where half the institution is saying one thing and the other half is saying another. That restricts us and adds risk to the communication from a marketing perspective. Harnessing that is a complex issue. Getting the institution's arms around that is a smart strategy. As I say in the book, it is much less important *which* decision is made, but that *a* decision is made. Otherwise, in a vacuum, chaos reigns."

> — Robert Rose, chief strategy officer, The Content Advisory,
> chief strategy advisor, Content Marketing Institute, author,
> co-host of *This Old Marketing* podcast

Content is an asset, not a commodity. When we start looking at our content as a product, with a life cycle and opportunities for constant improvement, that is when we start taking the step toward treating our content the way a media company treats its content: like it has inherent value.

Look at the big brands that are leaning into content marketing so much that they have become media companies. Lego, Red Bull, Amazon— these brands recognize the power of the content they create and leverage that content to engage, entertain, and inspire their audiences.

How Is Content Strategy Different from Content Marketing Strategy?

There is a difference between content strategy and content marketing strategy. Content strategy should guide the rationale behind all the content you distribute across all your channels, while content marketing strategy focuses on the content you are specifically creating to get a target audience to know, like, and trust you so they will eventually help you reach your goals.

Let's start with content strategy because content marketing strategy is something different. As defined by Kristina Halvorson in her book *Content Strategy for the Web*, "Content strategy is the practice of planning for the creation, delivery, and governance of useful, usable content." [1]

"Content is central in all the things that we do from marketing and communications across the board. When you do that well, the heart of that is your content strategy. Content strategy is when you clearly articulate your brand and the things that separate you and make you distinct. All the stories you tell should anchor back to the areas that make you distinct. If any other institution can tell this story, you shouldn't. Once you have a really robust content strategy that anchors around your brand it feeds all of your tactics. Life gets so much easier if you are a storytelling machine, and then you can take that content and push it out."

— Jamie Ceman, senior executive vice president, RW Jones Agency

When you add marketing into the mix, you now begin focusing on audience needs, motivations, and how you can establish a relationship with them. You want your target audience to get to know, like, and trust you through your content. You want them to connect with your brand and messaging. You want them to think, "These people are like me. They get me. And they want to help me solve my problems."

Next, you want to give your audience opportunities to engage. They can do so in a variety of ways: from consuming more content to sharing it. Then to requesting information, enrolling, or donating.

In his book *Content Marketing Strategy*, Robert Rose walks through various definitions, from business to strategy, to help frame his definition. "Content marketing strategy—a marketing discipline that is the sum of all the activities required to enable a business to consistently communicate in a way that creates tangible value for target audiences. It is what enables a brand to have not only a voice but also something to say that is worth listening to." [2]

"When I'm talking with an institution, I say, 'here's your brand platform, here's your more emotional connection stuff, and here are the thematic buckets that you need to talk about. Here are the recommended content pillars that all content across the entire institution should ladder up to.' And they say, 'What, like all content?' 'Yes, all content, you only talk about these things.' That is still a conversation I have. But what I have found is if we can get central to agree on content pillars, and then we can get interest from other areas across campus, the content pillars have legs and can travel a little easier."

— Corynn Myers, associate vice president, strategy planning,
SimpsonScarborogh

Yes . . . all content. At least all content that is being targeted for marketing use. But what content is not used for marketing? Think about our landscape of content. Course descriptions? They do not have to be dry, pedagogic recitations of every topic covered in a course. They can include stories from students, teaching assistants, faculty, and alumni.

There is not a piece of content that we create as higher education institutions that could not be leveraged for marketing. Every piece of content you create can include an opportunity to better connect with one of your audiences.

EPIC THOUGHTS

- A content marketing strategy should align with and ladder up to the institution's overall strategic plan and marketing plan. Every tactic employed and every piece of content created should intentionally connect to those higher-level plans.

- Having a well-defined content marketing strategy allows for more targeted tactics, clearer KPIs and goals, and better measurement of whether the content is helping reach those goals.

- Successful content marketing requires establishing a consistent brand voice across the institution, rather than having different areas convey conflicting messages. Getting alignment on core content pillars that all content should ladder up to is key.

EPIC RESOURCES

1. Kristina Halvorson, *Content Strategy for the Web* (New Riders, 2010), 32.

2. Robert Rose, *Content Marketing Strategy: Harness the Power of Your Brand's Voice* (Kogan Page, 2023), 22.

CHAPTER 3

Audience First

Lots of Audiences

One of the first things I did when I started my job in higher education was to make a list of all the audiences we were trying to target with our content. Not just the ones we were currently targeting, but all potential audiences that we could create content for. I ended up with more than 50 audiences.

These audiences included everyone from potential and current undergraduate and graduate students to potential and current faculty, staff, donors, alumni, government officials, and so many more. I was shocked. My previous job had been at a defense contracting company where we had a handful of audiences in each of the different sectors we covered, but nowhere near 50.

I knew we could not possibly create content to address and engage each one of those audiences, so we needed to begin by identifying the key audiences. You do this by going back to your strategy and determining which audience could have the biggest impact on moving you closer to completing a goal.

"You can't have a good strategy if you don't understand your audiences. Sometimes, that is the hardest part of all this. We have so many audiences we're trying to market to, including prospective students and their families, current students, parents, alumni, faculty, staff, and the world at large. That's a lot of different beasts to appease."

— Dave Tyler, director of university social media,
Rochester Institute of Technology

One of the biggest mistakes you can make when creating content is not having a specific audience in mind. Remember, "everyone" is not an audience. Yes, the content might be something that everyone should know, but as you are creating it, you must focus on your primary audience. Who is most likely to take action to help support your strategy by consuming your content and being moved by it? How do you figure out the needs and problems of your primary audience so you can create content that provides the most value? You listen to them.

"We can get tunnel vision and get so focused on content creation in our marketing campaigns that we can forget to take time and listen to what our audiences are saying and feeling."

— Harrison "Soup" Campbell, head of community experience, ZeeMee

To create successful content marketing, you must actively listen to your audiences. There is no one-size-fits-all approach to address multiple audiences with your content and still have it be relevant, valuable, and engaging.

We must be able to adapt our content and our messaging to address our evolving audience needs. We must also recognize that as our users consume our content, they are constantly learning and developing their understanding of who we are as an institution. The point of content marketing is to inform and inspire while creating lasting connections and building trust with each community we serve.

"Every college and university is like a small city, and you have to figure out what content is going to work for every neighborhood. That's just within the institution. Then you have external groups like alumni, the business community, and your donors. It can be a daunting task to figure out what resonates with these groups. You can't say the same thing to every audience the same way."

— Eddie Francis, brand strategy consultant/principal,
Edify Ventures, LLC, host of *I Wanna Work There!* podcast

As higher education marketers, we have unique access to our audiences in a way that many B2B and B2C companies do not. If we want to learn about our different audiences' needs, goals, decision criteria, and fears, we can often simply walk out onto the campus and talk to them.

This is the type of information we would try to collect if we were creating a persona. We then take that information and use it to inform how we create content, not only to help that audience but to engage with them in a way that connects on an emotional level. That is what relationships are all about—feelings.

"How do you have feeling come across in your content? The first thing is: feeling yourself. Start with your feelings, and then your audience's feelings will follow."

— Andrew Cassel, director of communications and science engagement,
Hubbard Brook Research Foundation

When we are creating content marketing, we need to know how we can make our audiences feel inspired, informed, or connected. What is it about this content that will matter to this audience? Start and end each piece of content you create by asking why it matters to your audience, how it will add value for them, and what feeling or problem you are trying to address.

"We have lost our imagination as an industry. We need to be thinking bigger about how we can meet audiences where they are [by] talking about things that actually matter [and]helping them move forward in their lives and careers, independent of us as institutions."

— Tim Jones, director, brand and integrated strategy,
SimpsonScarborough

The key to epic content marketing is to stay focused on adding value for the audience, not for your institution. Focusing on your audience first will benefit your institution long-term.

Pull Versus Push

Content marketing is one strategy to use within the larger marketing landscape. There is a time for paid advertising. There is a time to push your audiences to do something by reaching out with a direct call to action. But there is also a time to build connections and add long-term value through content and pull them into a relationship.

"I think content marketing and focusing on adding value to an audience over time is the only way you can create differentiation. If we just keep putting money into campaigns, all we're doing is renting an audience for about three months a year."

— Kyle Campbell, founder and managing director, Education Marketer

With the loss of third-party cookies, the restriction of access to data around our target audiences, and an ever-increasing focus on privacy and user consent, we need to consider alternatives to paid advertising.

"As the market gets increasingly crowded, paid advertising will become increasingly cost-inefficient. That means that non-paid efforts, including content marketing, will become increasingly important. Being able to reach, engage, and drive value for your audiences will be key to increasing awareness and driving action for all institutions across all segments of higher education."

— Seth Odell, founder and CEO, Kanahoma,
co-host of *Higher Ed Pulse* podcast

Paid advertising can be very transactional. Many younger audiences are savvy about how marketing works and how they are often being manipulated and directed through the language and messaging being thrown at them. They don't like it. Brands do not build trust with banner ads or paid social.

"We have a responsibility beyond just promoting our colleges and universities. We have a responsibility to help students consider college, get into college, find the right college, and finish college. If we're working in enrollment or marketing, that's our goal, even if they don't end up at our institution. I'm a true believer that we need to play a helpful and advisory role with students, not just a sales role."

> — Allison Turcio, assistant vice president for enrollment and marketing,
> Siena College, host of Enrollify's *The Application* podcast

There are so many ways we can help our audiences with our content. It is important that we think about all the ways we can reach them in order to provide that value. We have countless channels, platforms, and digital environments where we can reach our audiences.

We are also uniquely positioned to connect with some of our audiences IRL (in real life) with on-campus communications. I bet many brands would love to have that opportunity at their disposal.

"With all our new technology, we're always looking at those methods, but sometimes analog methods are the best. They're tried and true. Sandwich boards work. Posters work. Put a poster in a bathroom stall where you're trying to reach students because that's a captive audience. Put it in the elevators. I'm all for new technology, but do not overlook the analog methods that have always worked in the past."

> — Jenny Li Fowler, director of social media strategy, MIT,
> author of *Organic Social Media: How to Build Flourishing Online
> Communities*, host of Enrollify's *Confessions of a Higher Ed Social
> Media Manager* podcast

Regardless of where you put your content or how it gets discovered, it always comes back to providing value. That is why I look at content marketing as a pull strategy. You want your users to come along with you, learn with you, collaborate and engage.

"If there's one thing that colleges and universities have, it's content. And if there's one thing that our audiences want out of us, it's the ability to think and engage. I always think about the 90/10 rule. If you're thinking about content marketing, 90%, maybe 95% of the time, you should be giving, giving, giving. 5% of the time, you can end up saying: this is something we love bringing to you, we would love to get your support and help engaging with this. Many institutions have it completely reversed. Many brands have it completely reversed. But you don't build relationships by taking. It becomes, 'how do I provide something of value to you, that you think is important, that you see as critical, that fits our culture and our mission?' and then we give you that opportunity to help support it. If you look at the Edelman Trust Barometer, groups that people really want to hear from and trust are scientists, they're academics. We are all given this great gift that we can employ."

> — Paul Rand, vice president of communications, University of Chicago,
> host of *Big Brains* podcast

Targeting and Focusing

It is tempting to want to cast the widest net possible with your message. To reach everyone, answer all the questions, and solve all the problems.

That is a fool's errand. You really need to know and understand your audience, but also recognize that not everyone is your audience. There are people out there who will not resonate with your message and who will not be a good fit for your institution. You may get lucky and happen to solve some problems for them, but you want them to know if they are going to be a long-term fit for your culture and your values.

"It's about identifying who the mission-fit student is for your particular institution. When I talk about mission fit, I'm talking about who is going to graduate, succeed, and want to tell other people about their experience. I believe there are people out there for every institution that are mission fit, and there are enough of them who would meet the requirements of your yearly admissions goal, but the problem is the way we do our marketing. We don't identify the watering holes. We don't identify who that perfect mission-fit student is. We think that everybody needs to know about our marketing, and they simply don't. That illiteracy of marketing practices is a real challenge right now."

> — Bart Caylor, president and founder, Caylor Solutions,
> president, The Higher Ed Marketer, author of *Chasing Mission Fit*

The true power of content marketing comes in the fact that it is a long-term strategy. Especially in the higher education landscape because we have the opportunity to be a resource for our audiences for their entire lives.

Our prospective students can turn into full-time students, graduate students, alumni, faculty, leadership, and even donors. We can potentially connect with them and build a relationship for life.

"Content marketing aligns with relationship building and content maintenance. In higher education, we have to do a lot of awareness raising and trust building . . . and a lot of asking. And we have to continue to build relationships. Our messages are a constant drumbeat of why we matter and how we can fit into our constituents' lives. After graduation, our alma mater is a very insignificant part of your everyday life. You're not always thinking about it. So, my team works hard to think about what people are doing in their lives and how can we insert the university into that. That's what it means to meet them where they are. It's not, 'What channel are they using?' It's, 'What is happening today? What are they doing today?' Can your brand be part of that conversation or not?"

> — Ashley Budd, senior marketing director, Cornell University,
> co-author of *Mailed It: A Guide to Crafting Emails That Build
> Relationships and Get Results*

The most difficult thing to do with content marketing is to maintain focus on your audience. It is so easy to start slipping back into the trap of talking about ourselves to ourselves. That is one of the reasons that audience personas are so critical to an effective content marketing strategy. More on that in Chapter 9, "How to Create Epic Content Marketing."

Every piece of content needs to be talking to *one* primary audience.

"Anyone who is a creator knows the value of content marketing as a tool to start to make connections and build those relationships. But the pendulum can swing too far where it's all about us. When the content calendar is more important than the relationships and the connections, we're just checking another box."

— Harrison "Soup" Campbell, head of community experience, ZeeMee

Staying focused on what matters most to your different audiences can be difficult in higher education, especially when you have lots of messages, communications, and content you have to put out around deadlines, events, and activities.

This is when you need audience focus more than ever. These are regular and consistent opportunities to connect with your audiences and make it clear to them that you care and understand what they are going through and are trying to make it easier for them.

"Universities are cyclical, and I think you can use that to help figure out what your content strategy is. What are prospective and current students feeling and experiencing in August and September? There's going to be some nervousness; they're going to be unsure of what to pack and what to think about when it comes to terms of coming on campus. Look at it from the eyes of the student and the prospective student about what they're feeling in that cycle. I think that's a really good place to start."

— Carrie Phillips, chief communications and marketing officer,
University of Arkansas at Little Rock

A critical element in accomplishing this is planning ahead. You cannot wait until the week before an event to start thinking about how you want to talk about it. Your content calendar should be at least a full quarter ahead. Larger events will take even more time. Remember, even with all these planned events happening, there will be many others that will come up and throw a wrench into your planning. You need to be flexible and able to pivot when needed.

"Every quarter, we do a brainstorm session to generate relevant content ideas we want to ship out the following quarter. If you're starting in the new year, in that first week of January you would be planning for the spring months, April, May, and June. Your brainstorm should prompt your group to think about what they will be doing in the spring, in their daily lives. What words come to mind? What activities are they doing? I try to kick it off like we're going to time-travel to April right now, even though it's January, and ask what people need during that time.

You will hear things like, 'People are going to want to get outside. They'll be thinking about planting their garden. They're going to be doing spring cleaning. There's going to be commencement happening.' Then I kick people into breakout rooms to think about content for that time of year. This approach is a foolproof way to create content that is timely and relevant for your audience."

— Ashley Budd, senior marketing director, Cornell University, co-author of *Mailed It: A Guide to Crafting Emails That Build Relationships and Get Results*

Not only do you have to think about what different audiences will be doing and thinking about throughout the year, you also must think about what they will be doing and thinking about at different stages of their content journey.

You do not want to be delivering the same content to someone who is just getting to know your institution that you would deliver to someone who is ready to apply, engage, or donate. Your content calendar needs to be mapped chronologically but also needs to be tagged by funnel location to ensure you are connecting with people at all different stages of their journey.

"For institutions, one of the hardest things I have seen them have to deal with is the difference in audiences at different parts of their journey. They need to focus on the priorities of the business. And get a coordinated media strategy around what is prioritized to make sure that the platforms getting rolled out are not just responses to basically the needs of our various audiences, but rather prioritized against our business goals. Where can we add value to one very specific thing? One audience, one platform; focus and do it well, then expand."

— Robert Rose, chief strategy officer, The Content Advisory, chief strategy advisor, Content Marketing Institute, author, co-host of *This Old Marketing* podcast

Targeting and focusing on your audience is all about constantly asking "why" regarding your content. Why do they care? Why does this matter to them? Why does this fill a need? When it comes to identifying their needs, it is all about having the right information.

Use your data, qualitative and quantitative. Do surveys, ask questions, look at your analytics, do social listening, and use your resources. Identify the gap, then fill it with valuable content.

"Start with your audience. Find out their pain points. What are the things they would value getting help with? You shouldn't decide for them, you should go and ask. One of the things we found was that access to school and college counseling resources is not equal or equitable among all types of schools and all types of students. We decided that we could help fill that hole. We have expertise in college admissions—even if they don't end up at Siena, we can help students understand what courses they should take in high school for certain majors, we can help them understand how to craft an essay, and we review essays for students who don't even end up applying to Siena. That was one of the things we found in our market that was a need. Go find what your audience needs."

> — Allison Turcio, assistant vice president for enrollment and marketing,
> Siena College, host of Enrollify's *The Application* podcast

There is a fine line between creating content that is truly useful for a particular audience at a specific part of their journey, and creating content that you think should be useful. That is why data is so critical. Use your data to inform your decisions about what new content you should be creating and what existing content you should be optimizing, then pay close attention to what happens with that content. If it is working, look to create additional content that adds even more value.

If it is not working (and this is the important part), stop creating that type of content. Or switch it out for different content to try to fill that gap. Or look to see if there really is a gap. Sometimes you create content to fill a gap, only to discover that it is not actually a gap for your specific users. Always monitor to see if your content is performing. Do not just throw it up on a channel and move on to the next piece of content.

It is easy to fall back into the quantity trap. That is one of the pitfalls of vanity metrics. Low-value metrics like views and likes do have their place in tracking, but they should not be the only indicator of success. Look for ways to measure conversions and engagement on content. Create content with a clear indicator of what success should look like. This is especially important when you are telling stories because stories have the most potential to connect and motivate.

Think hard about the stories you tell before you tell them. Think about what part of that story will resonate the most with your audience and provide the most value. What angle is most likely to get them to do what you want them to do after they consume it? Is it commenting? Clicking a link? Filling out a form? Think about how you tell that story to make them want to take that action.

"We constantly have so much to communicate, and there is so much happening. Hence, what we are putting out there is often very underwhelming because we don't have time to build things that are a bit more outstanding. This is the exact opposite problem that a lot of industries have. They have to work to find stories to tell; we have to work to find the right stories to tell."

— Emanuel Díaz, head of content marketing, IE University

Once you find the right story for that audience and for that goal, you then need to think about what you are going to do with that story. Are you trying to educate, inspire, entertain, or all the above?

"How do we make this better for the people who are consuming it? How do we make it more meaningful, memorable, and useful? Or, just fun? Fun has a place in higher ed, I swear."

— Tim Jones, director, brand and integrated strategy,
SimpsonScarborough

Fun is not just for the people consuming your content and your stories – it should also be fun for the people creating the stories. If you are not having fun talking to your students, faculty, and staff and hearing their stories, you are not going to be able to make your audience have fun when they are reading them. You are not going to be able to connect with them with your content.

That is an important part of selecting the right stories as well. Having the data and empirical evidence around what types of stories and content perform well and help you reach your goals is not only critical for the creators when they are telling those stories, but also vital for the editors when they are selecting which stories to tell and when they are having conversations with stakeholders about why they should or should not be telling specific stories.

"The most important step is to be able to articulate those areas of distinction. A messaging map is a good way to do that. If you can't articulate that, then you have to cave to the pressure of people wanting you to tell their story. Every central office gets bombarded with, 'this faculty did this great research,' 'my department did this thing,' 'we won an award here,' and all those are great, but at the end of the day, you only have so many resources, and you can only do so many things. If you can clearly say, 'that is fantastic and maybe we can find some way to highlight that, but it's not a story that makes us distinct, therefore, we're going to have to pass on this one, but congratulations to you.' There are only so many hours in a day, and there are so many stories to tell, and you have to be able to anchor to something strategic."

— Jamie Ceman, senior executive vice president, RW Jones Agency

Make the most of the resources you have. Better to put out one incredible story that connects, delivers, and moves your target audience than to put out twenty pieces of mediocre content that no one wants to read and does not result in any beneficial outcome.

"Content marketing forces us to think about our audiences as whole and complex people, so it adds a lot more to the institution than just a new approach to marketing. It actually brings a whole new understanding and way in which we think about the people that are part of our community."

> — Tracy Playle, chief content strategist, Pickle Jar Communications, author of *The Connected Campus*

EPIC THOUGHTS

- Higher education institutions have many potential audiences, but content marketing efforts should focus on the key audiences that can take actions that have the biggest impact on institutional goals.

- Focusing content on a specific audience is critical. Develop audience personas, constantly ask "why" they would care about the content, and use data to identify and fill real gaps in addressing their needs at different stages of the journey.

- Telling the right stories will connect with the target audience and motivate them to take the desired action. Put resources into fewer pieces of outstanding content aligned with strategic priorities versus high volumes of generic content.

CHAPTER 4

Why Should You Use Content Marketing?

Content marketing takes time to work. It takes commitment. It is not the easiest marketing method to measure. There are dozens of other ways to market that use fewer resources and take less time.

I am not saying that you should not use some, or all, of those tactics. But content marketing provides an opportunity to grow an audience and create superfans in a way that few other marketing strategies can.

"Content marketing is the number one marketing tactic that should be employed by every institution. I think it gets to be more important the smaller the institution, especially since there's a difference between brand awareness and lead generation. Content marketing drives a lot more lead generation as opposed to brand awareness. I encourage a lot of smaller institutions to focus on content marketing."

— Bart Caylor, president and founder, Caylor Solutions, president, The Higher Ed Marketer, author of *Chasing Mission Fit*

There are so many ways to use content marketing to reach your strategic goals and stay aligned with your content marketing strategy. Whether you are a small community college looking to generate leads or a large research university trying to build brand awareness and maintain your reputation, content marketing can be an incredible resource for you. It always surprises me to see how many businesses and brands are leveraging content marketing and thinking about more integration of content marketing, while most institutions that I talk to are not even thinking about including content marketing in their efforts.

"Content marketing remains critical; it should already be critical. I don't think people take it seriously enough. It blows my mind that I still talk to clients today who are still having those same issues. How are we not further along?"

— Rachel Reuben Senor, vice president, account strategy,
OHO Interactive

Content marketing is not a trend, and is not only for big brands. It is not just about generating new student leads, attracting the best faculty, or getting more donations—it's about building a strong and recognizable brand that can handle the challenges we face as an industry.

By prioritizing content marketing, integrating it into your broader marketing landscape, and investing in it as a long-term strategy, you can position yourself for success and survival amidst all the challenges that we face.

"Content marking for higher ed is absolutely critical for the future success of institutions. I don't think there's another way to put it: it's mandatory. There is not a scenario where content marketing is a nice to have but not a necessary component of the mix. We see the conversations that are happening in the industry around consolidation and closures. If you don't have a strong brand reputation and you don't have any awareness in your institution, you're much more likely to face those sorts of circumstances and outcomes. Content marketing is a great way to retaliate against those threats and to push up value, meaning, and relevance to the audiences that matter most to higher education."

— Tim Jones, director, brand and integrated strategy,
SimpsonScarborough

We will talk more about the specific challenges higher education is facing in the next chapter, but the best defense any institution has against those issues is a strong brand. A strong brand comes from building relationships with your audience over time—which is where content marketing excels.

"The brand is what we are, not what we want to be."

> — Andrew Cassel, director of communications and science engagement, Hubbard Brook Research Foundation

Be Authentic

Authenticity trumps perfection when connecting with your audience. Content marketing gives us a unique opportunity to be authentic with our content. This is especially important on social channels and short-form videos, and for younger audiences, like Gen Z and Gen Alpha.

"The sooner we can get to a more human and customer-student focused approach to marketing, not institutionally focused, we'll all be better off."

> — Kevin Tyler, senior vice president and practice lead, Collaborative Communications Group

Our brand is the linchpin to authenticity. We have to embody the principles that we share publicly. One of the quickest ways to lose support and disappoint our audiences is to act in a way that counters the values and vision we have built our brand on.

"Having good content supports the brand and then the brand helps support good content. You can't just do one in isolation. I think sometimes, as higher ed marketers, we get too focused on very tactical things, and we don't spend enough time talking about what it means to be this institution. What is our brand? What are the things that we offer?"

> — Carrie Phillips, chief communications and marketing officer, University of Arkansas at Little Rock

By taking the time to clearly understand your institution's unique identity and finding the best ways to communicate that through your content in a meaningful way, you can build a brand that not only stands out but also stands for something.

We know that our audiences are looking for sources they can trust. Content marketing provides us an effective, consistent, and repeatable way to build that trust over time by telling stories that can only be ours and that showcase the expertise and experiences of our people.

"There will be a premium on creativity. That's an inevitability. That is going to be the differentiation point. Because we're competing against commodity content. There's going to be a premium on that in the ways that institutions shape their curriculums and their offerings, but also in the way that we outreach and connect with our audiences. The expectations we have of our audiences need to change. We need to meet them where they are, but don't leave them there."

> — Tim Jones, director, brand and integrated strategy,
> SimpsonScarborough

We are all on journeys. Those journeys may be professional, personal, mental, spiritual, or a variety of different areas. Our audiences are on journeys as well. They are all looking for guidance, information, and for validation that the steps they are already taking are the right ones.

Our content is often our first interaction with our audiences and thus our first opportunity to make an impression on them. Any piece of content can be the first item that a user sees from our brand. This is why it is so important to think about integrating the brand voice and values into everything we put out.

"Content marketing is essential to higher education institutions because choosing a school is a decision that is indeed very rational, but even more so emotional. It's imperative that our content stops just selling and starts being meaningful and inspiring to our audiences. Emotion will keep playing a pivotal role, and we must bare the soul of who our institutions really are and what we care for."

> — Emanuel Díaz, head of content marketing, IE University

We are asking for big commitments from our audiences. We are asking for years of commitment and struggle from our students, for mentally challenging and exhausting work from our faculty, and for maximum effort with minimal resources for our staff. We can help alleviate those challenges and make these requests worthwhile by sharing and helping through our content.

"If we want to capture people's attention, we have to say something worth their attention. We often make big assumptions about what that is, and then we are disappointed when they don't click through, they don't participate, they don't follow our call to action. And it's because we haven't made the effort to find something of interest to them."

> — Teresa Valerio Parrot, EdD, APR, principal, TVP Communications,
> co-host of *Trusted Voices* podcast

In the attention economy that we live in, our content must stand out. We are not just competing with content from other schools, we are competing for our users' attention with every brand, influencer, and content creator out there.

"We are in a stage right now where everyone is a media outlet and if you are not telling your story, providing value, or bringing awareness to what you're doing as an academic institution, you're missing the boat. We have to be aligned with industry trends. Companies, organizations, and nonprofits are using content marketing across the board. We have to be skilled in higher ed to not only do this to our external audiences, but also internally, with our staff, students, and faculty. If we're not investing in content, we are hindering ourselves and missing the opportunity to form connections, build communities, and reach the audiences where they're at. We don't have the luxury in higher ed to just sit on the sidelines. We need to be along the same lines, not just with industry, but even pushing the envelope and seeing how we could potentially lead in this area. It's a big task, but we'll see what we can do in higher ed."

> — Karen Freberg, professor of strategic communication,
> University of Louisville, director, The Bird's Nest Student Agency

Our content extends beyond our own digital landscape. Our brand can be mentioned by our advocates in so many different places, including social channels, discussion sites like Reddit and Quora, and communities on channels like Slack, Discord, and Circle. Active listening and regular searches on these types of channels can reveal all sorts of conversations that are happening about your institution.

"Authenticity is more important now than ever. Find the spaces where your fans are, the people who are already talking about you, the people who are excited to be there. Tap into those people and then have a campaign that is user-generated. Direct message them and ask if you can use [their content] on your channel. If they're already saying that you are their dream university, they will say yes in a heartbeat. More social media managers need to use listening and monitoring to find those fans, and tap into [their] genius and authenticity."

> — Jenny Li Fowler, director of social media strategy, MIT,
> author of *Organic Social Media: How to Build Flourishing Online
> Communities*, host of Enrollify's *Confessions of a Higher Ed Social
> Media Manager* podcast

Pat Flynn is a well-known keynote speaker, content entrepreneur, and author of several books, including *Superfans*. In *Superfans*, he outlines the process of taking a casual audience, converting them into an active audience, then a connected audience, and, finally, into superfans.

He has built his entire business following this model, and higher education institutions have an unparalleled opportunity to use it for ourselves. What other situation in a person's life do they spend money to live and be in a place for several years in a row? It is almost laughable that we do not do more to try to build this level of trust and depth of relationship with this captive audience. All we need to do is take advantage of every opportunity we have to make them feel special and feel heard. To let them know we are glad they chose us and will do everything we can to help them succeed.

"Content marketing is part of a relationship. Communication and marketing are often seen as one-way forms of communication. We are sharing with you, we are talking to you, we are presenting to you.

I think of content marketing as building a relationship where you first attract the person and then build a relationship so that there's engagement (and it doesn't have to be an active engagement). But you create an environment where others want to know more. Then, once you have a relationship, you need to ask yourself how you plan to retain that audience longer term. We usually think about a personalized relationship in enrollment management. Once students come to campus, how do other offices, including marketing and communications, keep ourselves in that engagement and retention mode so that we keep them engaged all the way through graduation and beyond? For a lot of institutions, that relationship ends the second students pay their first tuition bill. Content marketing is the totality of a student's experience with our institution, not just a sales job to get them in the door. We miss opportunities for connection if we think that it stops the second that they send in their acceptance."

— Teresa Valerio Parrot, EdD, APR, principal, TVP Communications, co-host of *Trusted Voices* podcast

Of course, this needs to extend farther than content marketing, but content marketing can help us establish transparency and openness with those audiences to let them know we are constantly working to make things better, easier, and more impactful for them.

Your superfans can be the most vocal and ardent supporters of your brand. They will do things like support you through crisis, recommend you to the world, and even get your logo tattooed on their bodies.

Build Trust

One of the biggest benefits of content marketing being a long-term strategy is that it allows you to build trust with your audiences by providing continual value. If you are consuming content online and read a post or an article that is useful or valuable, you might save or bookmark that page. However, until you get multiple pieces of useful content from one source, you probably will not subscribe or follow. That is where content marketing pays off. By gradually moving those casual audiences into connected audiences, you are expanding on your ability to create those superfans in the world.

"Content marketing is vital to show prospective students behind the curtain. For example, a video on a website course page of the lecturer talking about the course content, or a graduate talking about their experience, goes so much further than a page of text alone. Content marketing builds trust and authenticity and gives greater context for what the university stands for and what they have to offer students."

— Philip Smith, founder and CEO, Education Marketing Agency

You build trust by adding value: actionable, useful, relevant content that addresses the real needs of your audience. They need to know that you are as committed to their success as they are. Or even more committed, in some instances.

Much of the time, the content we create may not resonate with a particular audience. That is all right as long as we do not keep making more of that type of content, and instead learn from it and look at ways to update, change, or replace that content to generate more relevance and utility.

One of the things we say all the time in content marketing is "You are not your audience." Your audience does not care about you, your offerings, or your programs. They only care about how those offerings and programs will help them.

"We do this on the program side and the college admissions side and we do it in different formats. We do downloadable PDFs, and we also run live video chats. It's not about Sienna. We will have a Q&A chat about college essays, or how to develop your list of colleges that you're interested in. We hold it in the summer for about two weeks and call it College Application Bootcamp. We just email and text the students the next steps every day, getting them a little more prepared for when the common app opens on August 1. They're ready to start filling that out. We get about 1,000 students a year to do that."

— Allison Turcio, assistant vice president for enrollment and marketing, Siena College, host of Enrollify's *The Application* podcast

We can derail ourselves at any stage of our content journey by including content that moves away from being valuable and helpful and becomes transactional. Our audiences know that we have agendas and are trying to get them to take action, but they are willing to accept that as long as we keep helping them.

The moment they think that we are no longer focused on them and are just focusing on ourselves, they will go find another source of truth. It can take years to build relationships and mere moments to destroy them.

"When it comes to marketing, because the goal is butts in seats and not connection to hearts, it's a very transactional situation. If we could get past transaction and more to connection, I think that would serve us well."

> — Kevin Tyler, senior vice president and practice lead,
> Collaborative Communications Group

It is the move away from transactional content into valuable content that we need to focus on. Most marketers tend to think transactionally and focus on calls to action and ROI. There's nothing wrong with that, but content marketing is all about the connection, the relationship, and the value.

"Sometimes higher ed is focused on pushing messages out and providing information rather than saying, 'How can we use content to spark a conversation? How can we have a conversation and a dialogue and build a relationship?' We have the awareness and branding component down fine. We have our messaging, we have our videos, we have all of that. What is missing is: how do we use content strategically and creatively to bring them into our community so that they feel valued as part of our higher ed institution?"

> — Karen Freberg, professor of strategic communication,
> University of Louisville, director, The Bird's Nest Student Agency

Content marketing is a journey, for us and for our audiences. We must constantly be looking for ways to help them get where they are going and ensure they can find our content as they are asking the next question or solving the next problem they encounter.

It is not enough to simply make the content. We need to make sure we are putting that content in a place where our audiences will discover it.

"I always talk about content marketing in three phases: raise awareness, become liked and trusted, and then motivate action. I think colleges often go right to the endpoint. You can't become liked and trusted if all you're doing is telling someone how you want them to behave and be."

— Tim Jones, director, brand and integrated strategy, SimpsonScarborough

Along with putting out content to tell our audiences how to reach the next step along their path, we need to be sure that we are taking that path ourselves. We cannot tell our students and faculty that we want them to be bold and take chances if we are not willing to do so as an institution. Trust stems from authenticity. Being grounded in our values is more important than just having values.

"An issue with many higher ed institutions is that we sell something amazing, but when our students get there, the experience is drastically different and underwhelming. Under promise and over deliver, always."

— Emanuel Díaz, head of content marketing, IE University

EPIC THOUGHTS

- Content marketing is critical for higher education, especially smaller institutions, to build brand awareness, generate leads, and strengthen brand reputation to navigate industry challenges. It should be prioritized as a long-term strategy integrated into the broader marketing mix.

- Authenticity is key in connecting with audiences through content marketing. Institutions must embody their stated brand values and identity in everything they communicate. Showcasing the unique expertise and experiences of their people builds trust over time.

- Higher education has an unparalleled opportunity to build deep relationships and even "superfans" by making audiences feel heard, valued, and supported throughout their entire journey, not just as prospective students. Content should make them feel the institution is committed to their success.

- Content marketing allows institutions to gradually build trust by consistently providing relevant, useful content that addresses real audience needs, not just pushing promotional messages. The goal is shifting from transactional to relational content.

CHAPTER 5

Challenges to Higher Education

The higher education landscape remained relatively unchanged for centuries. As a matter of fact, the entire education landscape remained relatively unchanged. It was mostly a system of physically showing up at an institution of learning, sitting through lectures, reading material, doing homework, and then being tested on the knowledge that you had absorbed and could regurgitate.

Of course, there have been numerous changes, advancements, and evolutions of the system, learning methodologies, curriculum, means of instruction, and cost. But, in general, the mechanics remained fairly steady.

Some schools were even making a concerted effort at distance learning and online training, but, for the most part, those methods were dismissed as "less than" and were mostly viewed as substandard -- until 2020, when we were all forced into online and remote learning.

I spent 20 years of my career developing computer-based training (CBT—what we called it back in 1996) and online learning for B2B and B2C companies. Brands recognized the value of this type of training early on and have used it extensively to deliver training to large and repeat audiences.

Now that the Covid-19 pandemic has revealed that online learning can be effective and unlock entirely new audiences, more schools are beginning to lean into that evolution.

However, the issues higher education faces today may cause more change, upheaval, and disruption than anything the industry has experienced previously. Figuring out how to do marketing—and content marketing—in this era will be critical to educating the world on how we are changing.

"This can be a period of golden opportunity, a golden age, for higher education marketing, because our skills are so greatly needed for the challenges that we face right now. Our expertise is directly related to responding in effective ways."

> — Teresa Flannery, executive vice president and chief operating officer,
> CASE, author of *How to Market a University*

Change is difficult in higher education and that is an understatement. While institutions are constantly teaching our students and telling our researchers to innovate, explore, and experiment, the institutions themselves tend to be very comfortable (for the most part) with business as usual.

While businesses and brands are constantly evolving and looking for ways to innovate and be first to market, higher education tends to take a very different tack: watch and wait.

"The biggest challenge for higher ed is: how do we move our industry and our institutions at the speed that they need to be [at] to move along with industry?"

> — Karen Freberg, professor of strategic communication,
> University of Louisville, director, The Bird's Nest Student Agency

One of the problems with this approach is that while our pace of change may be slow, change is happening at a breakneck speed for our audiences. They see the impact that technology is having on the world. They see that the employment, economic, and political landscapes are changing daily. They want to figure out what their place is in this new world and determine who they can trust to help them adapt and succeed.

"You're not just competing with other colleges, you're competing with Amazon, Disney, and everybody else."

— Jeremy Tiers, senior director of admissions services,
Tudor Collegiate Strategies

Content marketing creates the mechanism and opportunity for us to deliver our message about how we are addressing these challenges, while also enabling our audiences to tell each other directly how we are changing and evolving to fit into the world and to help them fit in and find their place.

These are not challenges that we can ignore. We are already seeing the impact of these issues on our operations, our culture, and our leadership.

"Content marketing is life or death. I'm not being even a bit hyperbolic about that. Schools are closing, staff cuts can happen, and I'm trying to convince everyone that it's jobs like yours and mine that can go away if there's a bad year or two."

— Nate Jorgensen, senior director of marketing, Miami University

This chapter will explore a few of these threats and obstacles but there are many more that are affecting different schools, and we will continue to face other challenges over the next few years.

"The biggest obstacle to innovation and change is the *US News and World Report* rankings. Just give up on that stuff. What about the students? What about Gen Z? What are we doing to change? Where's all this entrepreneurial spirit we are supposed to have?"

— Mark Schaefer, executive director, Schaefer Marketing Solutions,
speaker, author, host of *The Marketing Companion* podcast

As individual institutions, it is difficult to come up with tactics or solutions to help us address many of these issues because many of them extend to the entire market, not just to our school. These are societal issues, global issues, and situations that are oftentimes out of our control. Yet, there are things we can do.

"I have this belief that content marketing for higher ed should be a collaborative exercise because our industry is under such strong attack. There's still an opportunity to differentiate, carve out a specialty, and build topical depth and density around certain ideas that lift up higher education and institutions at the same time. And I just don't see that happening as frequently as it should on campuses."

— Tim Jones, director, brand and integrated strategy,
SimpsonScarborough

As we move forward, it will become increasingly important that institutions adapt to face these threats while still maintaining our focus on our brand and values. Regardless of the format our education takes, we still need to ensure that it maintains the highest level of quality and impact.

"The biggest challenge to higher ed is the changing face of what higher education is and why we're stuck in this four-year idea. It is not that. It's smaller certificates that you could get studying remotely because you want to improve your life. It's people who want little, short courses. It's people who are older that want to go back.

We talk so much about first-generation students or people who are coming from underserved communities into the college experience and 'are we doing enough to create a world where they feel like they belong?' That's important, but you [also] have people who are coming back from the military who want to get some higher education to improve their lives after they have served their country. What's the community like for them on campus? What about people in their forties and fifties who might want a little education in botany so they could be better gardeners?

It's changing what higher education means that is the greatest challenge. We get so stuck in the status quo, we work so hard to keep the things that we know going, that we don't see the full potential of what it could be. Then we get those enrollment cliffs coming because we don't have the people we've been counting on all these years. And we're not opening our eyes and our minds to the other potential opportunities that are out there."

— Andrew Cassel, director of communications and science engagement, Hubbard Brook Research Foundation

Enrollment Cliff

Nathan Grawe, the author of *Demographics and the Demand for Higher Education*, claims that due to declining birth rates during the 2008 recession, the number of potential traditional college students is projected to decline by 15% from 2025 to 2029. This will primarily impact schools in the Northeast and Midwest and will most likely hit community colleges and regional public universities the most.[1]

College-going populations in the South, West, and Mountain regions are expected to see an increase in their potential student populations in this period.

"There are simply fewer college-age traditional students, and those students are choosing to attend college at declining rates. These demographics pose the greatest threat to higher education and will, unfortunately, force a wave of mergers and acquisitions that will change the landscape of American higher education."

— Elizabeth Scarborough Johnson, chairman, SimpsonScarborough

Besides the reduction in potential student numbers in some areas, schools are also facing more issues connecting with those audiences in ways that they typically have, due to increased regulations, privacy concerns, and access to student data.

"The biggest challenge is going to be finding an audience and generating enough interest among that audience to be able to achieve the enrollment goals set forth by the college. That has always been the challenge, but it's going to be astronomically more difficult to do because of privacy laws and the way organizations like the College Board are changing how you can communicate and connect with students. This idea of purchasing X number of names to be able to generate enough interest is going away. What are we going to do? How are we going to go to the students? How are you going to know who they are and where they are? That is going to be an epic challenge."

— Allison Turcio, assistant vice president for enrollment and marketing, Siena College, host of Enrollify's *The Application* podcast

Perception of Value

In a *Chronicle of Higher Education* report from 2012, 60% of Americans believed that a college education was worth the cost. Only 12% disagreed with that statement. In 2023, the same study was done and 56% of those surveyed believed that higher education was *not* worth the cost. The change in mindset was most evident among millennials and Gen Z, with more than 60% of those populations expressing skepticism about higher education.

"There are very powerful forces that are looking to undercut the good that higher ed can do in the world, the good that knowledge can do in the world."

— Georgy Cohen, director of digital strategy, OHO Interactive

While it can be difficult for some of us to comprehend doubts about the value of knowledge, it is bigger than that. It is also about the rising costs of tuition and increasing student loan debt; the belief that higher education is not preparing students with the practical knowledge and skills needed to succeed in the workforce; the increasing availability and need for careers in the trades.

"The biggest challenge to higher ed, in a word, is relevance. Knowledge is not the goal anymore. Knowledge cannot be the goal. It cannot be that the purpose of a higher education institution is to relay knowledge. That is simply undifferentiated."

— Robert Rose, chief strategy officer, The Content Advisory, chief strategy advisor, Content Marketing Institute, author, co-host of *This Old Marketing* podcast

I believe all of us who have attended a higher education institution can agree that the value of an on-campus education extends far beyond knowledge and includes the entire experience of leaving home and being (mostly) on your own for, in many cases, the first time in your life.

For some people it is about having that time for discovery, exploration, and soul-crushing homesickness. Or, for others, it is about the lack of any immediate authority, the independence, and the opportunities to make some really bad decisions.

College is a time for growth, for finding new friends from a much larger pool than you had in high school, and for trying new things. It is about learning how to communicate, how to work as part of a team, and how to use critical thinking skills that are needed in so many careers.

And yes—it is about the knowledge and the education as well.

"There are a lot of question marks about the value of higher ed and the cost of higher ed. But it's such an important part of society. Education transforms people, brings people together, and moves us forward. Education advances society in every field. At the end of the day, we're contributing to something that matters."

> — Dayana Kibilds, strategist, Ologie, speaker, co-author of *Mailed It: A Guide to Crafting Emails That Build Relationships and Get Results*, host of Enrollify's *Talking Tactics* podcast

Some careers require the specialized education that you can only receive (currently) from attending additional school beyond high school. I do not think any of us would intentionally select a surgeon who received all their education online or that was self-taught. There is inherent value in physically practicing the skills needed for your profession as part of your education.

"The biggest challenge is the rapid decline in people's perceived value of higher education. I think that we're vastly underestimating the risks that come with that and how fast it's plummeting. I think the enrollment cliff boogeyman is what we're focused on. If we're not paying attention to that value proposition piece, we are in so much trouble."

> — Jaime Hunt, chief marketing officer, Old Dominion University, host of *Confessions of a Higher Ed CMO* podcast

If the general public decides that higher education is not worth the cost and starts encouraging their children to try alternate career or education paths, institutions will, fairly quickly, start to scramble as they realize the impact this could have on us all.

Even though studies show that, on average, people with bachelor's degrees or higher have a higher employment rate and increased earning potential compared to those with only a high school degree, there are more ways to earn certifications and online degrees now than there ever have been.

"We are going to need to share with each other much more than we're typically willing to do. We need to start looking around and at ourselves and collaborate as an industry. I don't think we're going to correct the perception issue if we don't do that. That challenge is not going away unless we start thinking as an entity. Then it's up to us to figure out what is going to resonate, be distinctive, and work for our school."

> — Allison Turcio, assistant vice president for enrollment and marketing,
> Siena College, host of Enrollify's *The Application* podcast

While it will be important for institutions to promote the value of higher education as a whole, we will also see the increased importance of promoting the ways in which your institution is different and why it stands out for particular audiences.

"The decline in consumer confidence is the most concerning issue facing higher education. This is an industry-wide issue and one that will likely be felt across all non-elite institutions. Within the institutions themselves, there is going to be a growing need for differentiation. Being able to make the case for individual institutional offerings (aka selling the institution, not the industry) will be key."

> — Seth Odell, founder and CEO, Kanahoma,
> co-host of *Higher Ed Pulse* podcast

Technology Changes

There are more online opportunities to get a degree now than ever before. Our post-Covid world understands that online and hybrid degrees can be just as relevant to a potential employer as on-campus degrees -- at a considerably lower cost while providing much more flexibility to learners.

While slow to be adopted due to access and technical limitations, virtual and augmented reality (VR/AR) learning spaces are growing and are particularly useful in fields like medicine and engineering by providing "hands-on" experiences without the risks of making an irreversible mistake in real life.

As we see wider adoption and integration of AI and VR/AR technology, we have to start thinking about the future of learning when all the knowledge we need will be at our fingertips, or available by using a voice prompt to our personal assistant housed within our VR/AR glasses.

"From a marketing perspective, generative AI is certainly a learning challenge unlike any other, and it's changing how we approach work as a whole. Regardless of what technology challenges we face, though, I try to keep my team grounded by bringing the focus back to our audience. What is their journey, what are their goals at each step of that journey, and how can we support and engage them as a brand? We will always experiment with new tech, but we must remember to adapt to the technologies that help make us more efficient as a team and more effective in reaching our audiences."

— Joshua Charles, director of web strategy and technology, Rutgers Business School

While these technologies may change the way we learn and access information, it will still be up to us as the marketers and communicators to remain focused on our audiences and to understand the new challenges and opportunities they will face as these tools continue to change their lives.

"Schools could dive into using AI so quickly, and ultimately, be more disconnected from authentic, meaningful connection and relationships. No amount of AI technology can reproduce that amazing admissions counselor that every prospective student loves. Many schools may go down that path thinking that they are going to be able to be more uniquely personalized because they can leverage AI, and in effect [are] worse because it's just less authentic, less true, and less real."

> — Harrison "Soup" Campbell, head of community experience, ZeeMee

Shift in Need of Degrees by Employers

Several industries and companies are reducing or eliminating the requirement that their employees need to have a four-year degree. In 2022, 18% of jobs listed on ZipRecruiter required a bachelor's degree, and in 2023, that fell to 14.5%.

IBM reported that 50% of its US job openings do not require a four-year degree, and many of these tech companies are prioritizing apprenticeships, coding bootcamps, and vocational training.

"Some employers have begun removing degree requirements from their job descriptions, which calls the value of the degree into question that much more."

> — Eddie Francis, brand strategy consultant/principal,
> Edify Ventures, LLC, host of *I Wanna Work There!* podcast

As we see more shortages of qualified job candidates in industries like retail and hospitality, government, and financial services, we will see a continuing shift away from degree requirements to increase the talent pool.

During a conversation in the Bay Area Meetup group in 2023, Robert Rose said "I'm waiting for an oracle or somebody like that to buy or launch a university where they can actually capture that engagement or attention from a desired audience."[2] Following that up in my interview with Robert, he added, "The classic example of this is Schneider Electric and Energy University. As of 2024, they've put 500,000 people through Energy University in the last decade or so. That's about 30 times the number of graduates coming out of UCLA over the same period. The value of that is incredible. Look at brands like Google, Oracle, Microsoft, or Apple that are looking to create a younger cohort of people who think of them as an aspirational brand and create a different kind of relationship with them. It makes perfect sense."

Employee Retention and Recruitment

A survey from the College and University Professional Association for Human Resources (CUPA-HR) reported that more than 50% of the higher education staff members surveyed said they were somewhat likely to look for a new job in the next year.

"We can't retain the staff we have, we can't find quality people to fill the open positions, and the people left behind have so much work on their plates and lack expertise in all the things they are now being asked to do. Every time I talk to a marketing leader, they're like, 'Oh, I know, I need to go figure out AI, but I don't have the time to do it.'"

> — Mallory Willsea, VP marketing, Element451,
> chief strategist, Enrollify, co-host of *Higher Ed Pulse* podcast

The biggest reasons cited by these respondents included compensation, ability to work remotely, career advancement opportunities, looking for a new challenge, or wanting a new supervisor.

Almost 25% of employees claimed they did not feel recognized for their contributions, and 40% felt unable to address problems or issues at work.

"At a lot of HBCUs, the directive becomes, 'I need you to do this.' And if the employee has trouble understanding what to do, it becomes, 'We hired you because you said you could do it. Since you can't do it, I think we need to get rid of you.' You don't agree on expectations, and a lot of folks are notoriously bad at understanding what exactly marketing is. A lot of them think they have a marketing and communications area when what they really have, and what they really want, is a brand management and communications area."

> — Eddie Francis, brand strategy consultant/principal,
> Edify Ventures, LLC, host of *I Wanna Work There!* podcast

Lack of clear communication between employees and managers can cause frustration, misunderstandings, and, eventually, turnover. Oftentimes, someone will leave their position and need to be replaced, and the new hire that comes in will lack the varied set of skills the previous employee had learned over years of performing multiple jobs or skills because there was no one else available to take those things on.

When trying to replace an employee with a versatile skill set, institutions will often not be able to compete with salaries from other markets.

While many higher education professionals cite the lack of a career advancement path, they are often just looking to increase their skills and have more professional development opportunities.

"The biggest challenge for most marketing teams is bandwidth. They are also not often incentivized to stay up-to-date and on-trend, and they are usually completely slammed. They don't have enough staff or time, they're exhausted and often don't want to use their personal time for professional development. Bandwidth will continue to be an ongoing challenge until senior leadership understands the strategic importance of marketing, how integral it is to everything they're doing, and that they need to fund it operationally and human resource-wise to take their school to the next level and help get them through the demographic shifts. One of the first areas to get cut in the department's budget is professional development. Marketers have to be really self-driven, and if they are self-driven, it's because they are already thinking about their next opportunity beyond that school, beyond that role."

— Rachel Reuben Senor, vice president, account strategy,
OHO Interactive

With all the challenges facing higher education, institutions will have to find ways to change to deal with those obstacles. For some people, that continual changing and adapting will be a challenge they will not want to take on. Especially some of the more seasoned and experienced people who will be even more difficult to replace.

"Change management is going to be almost impossible for a lot of people; they're going to get overwhelmed, and they're going to say, 'I'm out.'"

— Bart Caylor, president and founder, Caylor Solutions,
president, The Higher Ed Marketer, author of *Chasing Mission Fit*

Politicization

Higher education institutions are becoming increasingly polarized politically. There has been increasing partisan disparity in the confidence in higher education.

In a recent Gallup Poll, confidence in the value of higher education among Democrats dropped from 68% of respondents in 2015 having a "great deal" or "quite a lot" of confidence in higher education down to 58% in 2023. For Republicans, the 2015 numbers dropped from 56% down to 19% in 2023.[3]

"The politicization of higher ed should be a real concern for everyone in the industry. The recent events related to the presidents of Harvard, MIT, and Penn in addition to the increasing and aggressive involvement of state governments in higher ed are bellwethers that suggest colleges and universities will need to rally to defend and promote their missions, visions, and values in the coming years. Combine this with the trend toward the rejection of facts and data [and] it's easy to begin feeling as if the very scaffolding upon which the entire concept of higher education is built is unsteady."

— Elizabeth Scarborough Johnson, chairman, SimpsonScarborough

This reduction in confidence is causing a variety of changes to higher education, especially in states that tend to be more conservative. From laws being passed about what can and cannot be taught, to battles over boards of trustees and leadership positions, political agendas are becoming more prevalent and obvious across many campuses.

Self-Created Challenges

Along with these larger social issues we are facing in higher education, we often create our own challenges due to our internal structures or traditional methods of operating.

Silos

We cannot talk about challenges to higher education institutions without talking about silos. One of the topics you can always expect to come up at any higher education conference, or within any discussion among higher education professionals, is silos.

Something about the way that institutions have developed and traditionally functioned has led to the creation of numerous segmented groups who do not communicate regularly or openly.

These silos can be a huge obstacle for higher education content marketing.

"You can't do content marketing in a silo. The resources that you are providing your audience are probably not being developed by your team. If you are on the marketing communications team, you don't have insight into the pain points of the student journey the same way our admissions team does. We need to partner with our admissions team to understand what those look like. We need to partner with our career and leadership teams to understand what sort of things our students are facing out in the real world in the business landscape. Nobody has the full picture, so you have to work together."

> — Jackie Vetrano, assistant director, prospect management and
> marketing, UNC Kenan-Flagler Business School

Lack of clear communication between teams and groups who are putting out marketing or communications content can cause misalignment, confusion, and duplication of effort. It is easy to blame someone else for issues within their silo if you do not have any visibility regarding the issues or challenges they are facing.

"We keep everyone so segmented in their divisions, and it's easier to point blame. Students aren't engaged; that's a student affairs problem. Students aren't enrolling; that's an enrollment or marketing problem. No matter the size of the institution, we have to approach this holistically."

> — Josie Ahlquist, Dr. Josie Ahlquist, Inc.,
> digital engagement and leadership consultant

Centralization is a dirty word to many folks in higher education. People do not want to give up control. They do not want to have to get approval before they send that next newsletter or post that next story or social post. No one else knows their goals, audiences, or desired results as well as they do, so why should anyone else have input into what they are doing?

"We are fighting an inherent decentralized process of generating content in the Academy that, as part of its culture, says that academic freedom is really important. That is often interpreted to extend to members of the staff as well. Different teams can say what they want about their part of the university without thinking about coordinating in ways that are going to make it more effective. And one of the biggest challenges is identifying which parts of the institution should be responsible for primary communication with particular audience segments. If that could be coordinated or established in a more effective way, it would make content marketing a lot easier than it currently is."

> — Teresa Flannery, executive vice president and chief operating officer, CASE, author of *How to Market a University*

A few years ago at the University of Rochester, we did some research into video production across the entire institution. We had several groups with their own video producers, editors, and equipment; several groups that were outsourcing to agencies for the work; and even more groups who just were not undertaking video projects because they did not have the budgets or resources.

We did an exercise to scope the cost of having one centralized video production team that would be able to handle all the projects that various groups had mentioned. It included combined equipment, ownership of all the video assets, the ability to coordinate multiple shoots to save time and resources, and fewer overall personnel costs. Not to mention the insights into all the different initiatives that were going on across the institution.

The final numbers revealed there could be considerable savings. Leadership was impressed by the figures, but the groups that had their own teams were not willing to dissolve those teams and be unable to produce the videos they needed when they needed them. So, we ended up staying with our current model, but we have managed to increase communication and collaboration between the different video teams to help alleviate much of the duplication of effort.

"Marketing, branding, and storytelling have to be as centralized as possible because higher ed doesn't have the budgets that you have in retail to spend your way out of problems or spend your way to fame. Consistency matters. Speaking with one voice matters. The most successful schools are going to have marketing and communications 60 to 70% centralized, with really great talent adjacent in the major units, but they all work together."

> — Bill Faust, president, Ologie

Silos contribute to brand confusion because users do not understand that your entire digital landscape is not integrated. They may not understand why they might be seeing different marketing messages and content across your website or social channels.

Why are they seeing the same content in two different newsletters they receive on the same day? This typically happens because teams are not talking to each other enough and not sharing across the silos.

"One of the first things I do is look at the organizational structure. If there is a PR team on one part, other content folks sitting elsewhere, a web content team, and an athletics content team -- I know it's highly unlikely that they are talking. I always look at the org structure because that's usually a big telltale sign of there not being collaboration."

> — Rachel Reuben Senor, vice president, account strategy,
> OHO Interactive

When you look at brands doing successful content marketing, one of the first things they address is how to create consistent messaging and ensure collaboration between groups. When Jessica Bergman, vice president of content and customer marketing at Salesforce, was implementing their content marketing initiative, she placed content strategists into every content team across the business. All those content strategists worked within those teams but reported to her. Thus, she was always aware of what initiatives each group was working on, and those strategists helped to ensure that the content was aligned with the overall mission and values.

"We have been set up and are structured to service an industry that no longer exists, and we haven't caught up to the current market and consumer demands. I think the biggest issue is how we are structured to support and bring that level of experience and customer service, and then higher ed, in general, is not willing to pay well for expertise. They're not willing to get outside the belief that news is content and is the only collateral content that exists. That is not a thing. There's a level of not understanding the value of content, what it brings, and not resourcing it properly."

> — Rachel Reuben Senor, vice president, account strategy,
> OHO Interactive

Understanding the importance of consistent communication across silos is often an issue that is overlooked by leadership. Senior leadership at the institution must recognize the importance of overcoming this siloed approach, and leaders within the different areas must understand the benefit of collaborating with other teams.

"In higher ed, there seems to be a lack of value in the practice of marketing and the people and resources dedicated to it, and not being willing to do a top-down force of, 'You must centralize, you must work together.' That's all it would take to do that."

> — Corynn Myers, associate vice president, strategy planning,
> SimpsonScarborough

Difficult Processes

Outdated infrastructure makes it problematic for audiences to complete the action you are requesting of them. Whether we are talking about the enrollment process across the different schools within your organization or the hiring process for new staff or faculty, we tend to limp along with poorly constructed systems that feature horrible user experiences because that is what we have in place currently and it would be too costly or time-consuming to update.

"The amount of service and touchpoints required for students to get what they need is really high. We have all these pass-through places.

You talk to financial aid, you talk to advisors, you talk to faculty. There are so many people involved in that. It becomes a challenge."

— Myla Edmond, senior vice president, RW Jones Agency

I wish there was a way to track across an entire institution how many times potential students, staff, faculty, or alumni simply gave up on whatever task they were trying to accomplish because our environment made it unnecessarily difficult to complete.

Culture

Our culture within higher education can often be problematic if it does not align with our brand, our values, and our strategies. Many schools have a culture that is resistant to change, has siloed approaches, and reflects different stakeholder needs. Yet when you look at their values and strategies, they talk about innovation, collaboration, and community.

"Culture eats strategy for breakfast."

— Peter Drucker

It is confusing to our different audiences when they hear us tell them one thing, but then do not practice or embody that same thing in our actions.

Institutional leaders need to be constantly looking for these discrepancies as they are making decisions, approving plans, or reviewing messaging.

"It's difficult to [achieve] change when there are a lot of people involved who need convincing, who don't understand and have their own stuff happening. It's easier to fall back into best practices. Higher ed has difficulty changing because we're always comparing ourselves to other people. Being a leader in any space has great risk involved, and higher ed is highly risk-averse. Change is risk, and higher ed does not like that."

— Andrew Cassel, director of communications and science engagement, Hubbard Brook Research Foundation

We must look outside our market for inspiration and benchmarking. Always comparing ourselves against other higher education institutions is a surefire way to not differentiate ourselves or to push ourselves to embody our values.

"Higher education institutions often look to other higher education institutions for ideas. When we're all looking to each other, we're all doing the same thing. That is a recipe for stagnation. As an industry that is tasked to prepare people for the future of work, we need to evolve. If we are tasked to prepare the world for the future of work, and we are not willing to adapt to the future of work, we are doing the wrong thing."

> — Kevin Tyler, senior vice president and practice lead,
> Collaborative Communications Group

Resources/Budget

Higher education is typically known for having smaller budgets and limited resources. Unless you have a large athletic program or are an elite institution with significant endowments, you are probably constantly up against issues with finances and personnel.

This can become even more problematic if your institution uses a chargeback methodology where every transaction between different teams becomes financial. This is just another way to create walls between groups and to build those silos up even more.

"Some institutions have central marketing set up as a paid service, so you are basically competing against outside agencies and consultants for work. This can create an adversarial relationship and bidding wars within your own institution."

> — Corynn Myers, associate vice president, strategy planning,
> SimpsonScarborough

EPIC THOUGHTS

- Higher education is facing unprecedented change and disruption, including declining enrollments due to demographic shifts, skepticism about the value and ROI of degrees, new technologies reshaping how and where learning happens, and increasing politicization.

- Authentically communicating how the institution is evolving to address these challenges and provide value to students will be critical.

- Significant internal challenges, including siloed departments, outdated processes, change-resistant cultures, and limited resources, make it difficult for institutions to collaborate on consistent messaging and adapt to external threats.

- Turnover and understaffing in higher education marketing and communications roles (driven by compensation issues, lack of remote work and advancement opportunities, and burnout) pose additional hurdles to executing strategic content marketing.

EPIC RESOURCES

1. Nathan Grawe, *Demographics and the Demand for Higher Education* (John Hopkins University Press, 2018).

2. Robert Rose, "Marketing IS Content Marketing," Bay Area Content Marketing Meetup, October 25, 2023, YouTube video, 49:59, https://www.youtube.com/watch?v=yRQpdIcdJPw&t=2548s..

3. Megan Brenen, "Americans' Confidence in Higher Education Down Sharply," Gallup, July 11, 2023, https://news.gallup.com/poll/508352/americans-confidence-higher-education-down-sharply.aspx.

CHAPTER 6

How to Use Content Marketing in Higher Education

In the last chapter, we discussed many of the challenges that face us in higher education. In this chapter, we are going to talk about how content marketing can help us overcome some of these challenges and others.

Of course, the first issue is that leadership often does not understand what content marketing is and what their expectations should be, therefore they do not realize that content marketing can help alleviate some of these issues.

"The main challenge is that higher ed thinks it understands what content marketing is, assumes it's all those wonderful assets it publishes on its social channels, and it ticks that box. But I could probably count on two hands the number of institutions that use content as a proper strategic asset."

— Kyle Campbell, founder and managing director, Education Marketer

We will talk more about getting leadership buy-in and understanding of content marketing in Chapter 9, "How to Create Epic Content Marketing."

"Content marketing is an untapped means of marketing in higher education."

> — Jackie Vetrano, assistant director, prospect management and
> marketing, UNC Kenan-Flagler Business School

How Is It Different From B2B or B2C?

We can learn a lot from looking at how B2B (business-to-business) and B2C (business-to-consumer) brands are using content marketing, but first we must realize that there are important differences in implementation because there are fundamental differences in our structures, audiences, and outcomes.

"I think part of it is the purchase cycle. We are a service industry, and the purchase cycle for our consumers of prospective students is a little longer [than traditional B2B versus B2C]. In a service industry model, that makes it tougher for people to see the direct line between a sixteen-year-old who's searching, 'What should be in my college essay,' and stumbling upon an article on temple.edu, and how we get them to apply to Temple University. It's a squiggly, squirrely line between those two things. I think that's part of the challenge, and part of the reason why we are still in our infancy as an industry."

> — Angela Polec, vice president for strategic marketing and
> communications, Temple University

Other industries with long purchase cycles use content marketing. Before I came into higher education, I worked for a defense contracting company, and we had extremely long purchase cycles. However, we typically had well-defined audiences and lots of preexisting relationships with those audiences.

"Our audiences are less well-defined than B2B and B2C brands. Typically, for a B2B, you are very clear about who you are trying to market to, and even in B2C, you have a picture painted of your ideal customer. But in higher ed, we have so many stakeholders. Even within our prospective students, we have traditional-age freshmen, transfer students, adult learners, returning students, military students, online students, working parents; any human being on Earth is a potential audience. And it's hard to craft content that meets all their needs."

> — Jaime Hunt, chief marketing officer, Old Dominion University,
> host of *Confessions of a Higher Ed CMO* podcast

Because of the number of audiences we have, and the number of messages we need to deliver at so many points in their individual content journeys, it is easy to get off course when doing content marketing for higher education.

This makes it more important than ever to have clear audiences for your content, specific user journey maps, and measurable results.

"Strategic content marketing is important, and there are some institutions or organizations that try to throw all the content in all the different places"

> — Josie Ahlquist, Dr. Josie Ahlquist, Inc.,
> digital engagement and leadership consultant

Most brands have a fairly clear understanding of the features and benefits of their products. With traditional marketing, that is all they talked about: how great their products were. Once they got into content marketing, they had to make the switch to talking about the problems their users were trying to solve and the questions they had in the areas where their products or services could help.

Higher education content marketers must be very intentional about the content they are creating because it is easy to confuse audiences and mix messages, or to not address the right problems or questions of that specific user.

"Content marketing may be more important for higher education now than for any other industry because higher ed has a product problem, it has a positioning problem, it has a brand problem. And it's a big problem. It's a luxury good that, in many ways, has not lived up to the luxury brand idea. There are a lot of questions these days about, 'Why do I need this? Am I getting value for my money?' The opportunity for higher ed is to create a deeper level of trust by creating a relationship with an audience that starts to know and trust the brand of higher ed. It's one of the product groups or verticals that need content marketing more than just about any other."

> — Robert Rose, chief strategy officer, The Content Advisory,
> chief strategy advisor, Content Marketing Institute, author,
> co-host of *This Old Marketing* podcast

Like most content marketing programs, the shift comes when you start thinking of your content as your product. You are not selling your knowledge transfer to potential students, you are selling the outcome of the education and the impact that it will have on your user. Your content is the product they consume to see that impact and realize it is what they want.

Like any product, you should be constantly trying to improve and innovate with each piece of content so it better delivers your message and resonates with your audience.

"There is certainly a role for marketing and communications to play in helping institutions adapt to the realities challenging the industry. Delivering a focused and authentic brand message to target audiences through the right channels is essential. But a strong marcom program must be combined with better strategy across the institutional enterprise. For example, many institutions just need to reconsider their business model. All the marketing in the world isn't going to help an institution that is not offering the programs and experience their target audiences want. We can't continue to have almost complete separation between the development of new programs and the marketing department. We hear from our CMO clients all the time that faculty will create a new degree program and then run to marketing six weeks before launch and tell them to 'get students.' The marketing function needs to be fully integrated into the development of the experience institutions are offering; it can't continue to be perceived as the office that produces ads or brochures or landing pages."

> — Elizabeth Scarborough Johnson, chairman, SimpsonScarborough

Enrollment Cliff

For schools that will be most impacted by the enrollment cliff, there are several ways to address this. First, start by focusing on the retention of current students, identifying and promoting programs that are in demand within your target audience, and begin targeting nontraditional students who may not be considering higher education.

"If you are prepared to teach different kinds of people, you are not going to experience an enrollment cliff. The world will continue growing around the industry if it doesn't get up and start shaking off the dust and moving in a direction that is intentional and innovative. The space has enjoyed this position for so long, it thinks that it can't fail. I would be the first to tell the industry, that is not true. If the industry can't talk about itself in a way that people can understand, but someone else can, why would we not go over there? The idea that higher ed will never have challenges, which is what people seem to think, is false. And that will show itself."

> — Kevin Tyler, senior vice president and practice lead,
> Collaborative Communications Group

Look at your retention data for your existing students to see what the primary factors are that are causing them to leave. Look for opportunities to create content that is helpful for them and can better assist them in dealing with their problems, discover resources they did not know existed, or find communities of support that induce a stronger sense of belonging and connection.

"Educational institutions are a gold mine of pioneers, free thinkers, and original thought leaders. It is the higher education marketer's duty to harvest this valuable and compelling knowledge and distribute it amongst the public to attract, acquire, or engage a clearly understood target audience. It is how institutions of all sizes can safely navigate the demographic enrollment cliff."

> — Chris Rapozo, marketing specialist, Hannon Hill,
> host of *Marketing Tales* podcast

Examine trend data within your institution and region to identify the most in-demand skill sets related to your offerings and create content that addresses the opportunities and requirements within those areas.

Showcase how your graduates have changed their lives and solved the problems they were facing.

"The education consumer is not just the seventeen-year-old heading off for a life-changing event on campus. It is the working adult, it's the person who put their life on hold for the military and now they're coming back. It's the person who doesn't want a coming-of-age experience, they just want an education. It's the person who just needs a few certificates to get to the next level, they don't need a four-year degree."

— Bill Faust, president, Ologie

Any time we are faced with challenges, we have the ability to innovate, shift our focus, and think differently. The enrollment cliff is exactly what we need to expand our typical audience and think about who else could benefit from what we offer.

"In terms of the enrollment cliff, we need to come together holistically as higher ed. We need to collaborate. We need to go to businesses and say, 'How could we do collaborative partnerships and programs to create a whole new degree program that would be beneficial, relatable, and useful?' At the end of the day, higher ed is all about learning the basics of how to be a student of life, how to learn, how to think critically, how to be a good citizen, and how to have knowledge of all these different disciplines. And that will still be important. We still need higher ed, we just need to adapt and be agile."

— Karen Freberg, professor of strategic communication, University of Louisville, director, The Bird's Nest Student Agency

Perception of Value

The only way to address the shifting perception of the value of higher education is by telling stories detailing its impact.

The stories should be more than just how someone got their dream job or what programs they studied; it has to showcase the growth, change, and feeling experienced when you overcome all the obstacles in front of you through hard work, determination, and persistence.

And the stories need to speak to your audience.

"When it comes to navigating the perception of value for higher education and recognizing that this is a challenge that goes well beyond communications and marketing, one thing that I think we can do more is lean into the transformative power and impact of higher ed in our storytelling. We can tell more stories showcasing first-generation students whose lives were changed by getting a degree. We can tell more stories about the families living fuller, healthier lives due in part to new medical research from our faculty. And a whole lot more. Focus on people, focus on impact.

We also need to think bigger. Our audience is society as a whole, but we need to connect with people from all backgrounds and experiences on a personal level. That means telling personalized stories where people can see themselves in those experiences. On top of that, we need to communicate beyond our traditional channels to meet people where they are—in the spaces where they consume information and in the language they prefer.

The challenge is complex, multifaceted, and bigger than any one organization. But starting with the communities in which we serve, there are opportunities for communications and marketing teams to influence the perception of higher education for the better."

> — Joshua Charles, director of web strategy and technology,
> Rutgers Business School

It is important to tell the entire story, not just the learning and education portion. People know that is what you get at college; we have to show them all the potential things you can get.

"College is about so much more than academics and career preparation. It's a time to forge meaningful relationships, build your confidence, and, let's face it, have so much *fun*. Be it through joining clubs or studying abroad, it's about embracing adventures that help shape who you are."

— Melissa Fiorenza, vice president of content strategy,
CCA | Creative Communications Associates

The stories are bigger than getting a degree and getting a job or winning an award. The stories are life-changing, they are evolutionary, they are stories of growth and understanding.

"There are too many ways to attain knowledge. I can go take an MIT course for free. If I want the knowledge, I can go get it. What I can't get are all those other benefits that the classic university or higher education institution gives me. How to work with others, how to be social, how to learn, how to think. How do you use wisdom to bring experience and knowledge together to make better decisions in life? Those are the things that the higher education experience provides to you. Knowledge is simply the by-product of that. You're selling the experience of the university, not the benefits in terms of, 'You'll be smarter when you leave, and you will get a better job.' The new students are not finding relevance in that anymore, and they don't believe it. This is where content marketing comes in. They don't trust, and they don't believe the experience is worth it. That perception has to be changed. That belief has to be changed. Content marketing and storytelling are perfect vehicles for this. It's not that the experience of the university will make you a better businessperson or a better worker; it will make you a better person. That is the real value."

— Robert Rose, chief strategy officer, The Content Advisory,
chief strategy advisor, Content Marketing Institute, author,
co-host of *This Old Marketing* podcast

Telling stories of transformation should be a fundamental part of your content marketing strategy. The content should all tie back to your brand and support your mission and values. Consistently sharing this type of content will create awareness around your brand as users continue to see more and more content that is useful for them; content that also showcases how your institution is leading the way with how you think about these topics and the way you prepare your audiences to contribute to society. Every piece of content is an opportunity to share your brand and establish its importance.

"If you do not have an established brand that can stand this barrage against value, you might crumble."

> — Jenny Li Fowler, director of social media strategy, MIT,
> author of *Organic Social Media: How to Build Flourishing Online Communities*, host of Enrollify's *Confessions of a Higher Ed Social Media Manager* podcast

Shift in Need of Degrees by Employers

More and more, employers are finding that the college graduates they hire lack the real-world skills required to do their jobs.

"The issue that worries me is the perceived value of higher ed. The cost continues to skyrocket, there are other unique avenues into the job market, and many [employers] are dropping the formal degree requirement. Colleges and universities should make more strategic connections with corporations and businesses."

> — Harrison "Soup" Campbell, head of community experience, ZeeMee

Content marketing can be used to share resources with students and make them aware of internship opportunities, soft skills training, micro-credentials, partnerships with businesses, and other ways they can improve the skills that employers are looking for.

"I think of content marketing as the bridge that helps connect our content to the needs of our audience at each step of their journey. That's important in higher education because every organization and every message needs to stand out in our crowded market. Students have no shortage of colleges and universities to engage with, plus the sea of education opportunities offered through Coursera, LinkedIn Learning, Codecademy, and other companies."

> — Joshua Charles, director of web strategy and technology,
> Rutgers Business School

Just because your institution may not have a specific program that would be beneficial to your students does not mean you should not promote alternative options. Some institutions even have partnerships with different online course providers to give their students access to supplemental training and certificates that will be valuable to them when they enter the job market.

"The development of virtual learning spaces will not, in my opinion, replace in-person learning experiences. I believe strongly that there will always be a demand for people to gather in person and learn from experts. Virtual opportunities will complement in-person ones and expand educational options to new audiences. Access to higher education will improve, which will only serve to strengthen the industry."

— Elizabeth Scarborough Johnson, chairman, SimpsonScarborough

Employee Recruitment and Retention

While our employees are critical members of our institutional infrastructure, they are often overlooked as content marketing audiences.

It is just as important to provide them with resources, acknowledge their challenges, and share their stories as with any other audience. Maybe even more than some other audiences because they provide the framework upon which everything else functions.

Creating this connection and building a relationship starts from the moment of hire. It actually begins with the recruitment, application, and interview process, but our first big opportunity comes during onboarding, which is often an inconvenient and unhelpful process.

"Everyone is responsible for recruitment and retention, from the president, to faculty, to marketers, to admissions."

— Jeremy Tiers, senior director of admissions services,
Tudor Collegiate Strategies

When it comes to our employees, we are the community they belong to. If they do not feel welcomed, valued, or recognized, they probably will not stay. Then we must start the process all over again.

"We have to reimagine how we onboard new staff and be way more intentional. The higher ed workforce is getting younger, and they have way more options than they did 10 years ago. It's not like we're paying great either, so we have to find more people who see the value in this work and find it rewarding and fulfilling."

— Jeremy Tiers, senior director of admissions services,
Tudor Collegiate Strategies

Consistently connecting with your internal audiences is critical. To foster feelings that they belong and are welcome, you must be transparent. Tell them about challenges being faced and addressed by leadership, show why certain decisions are being made, and showcase how we are constantly looking for ways to improve their situations and make their jobs easier.

"Constantly reminding people of where they are and why they are there is valuable. At the end of the day, even people who get paid the lowest salaries want to know that they are in the right place. If the institution isn't putting something out there as a constant reminder of why you want to be there in the first place, you are missing opportunities."

— Eddie Francis, brand strategy consultant/principal,
Edify Ventures, LLC, host of *I Wanna Work There!* podcast

Understanding your internal audiences is often easier than your external audiences because you have so much data on them. Leverage the information you have to deliver more relevant, useful, and valuable content to them.

Spend time looking for resources to help them, opportunities that they can take advantage of, and professional development programs they can participate in.

"If you are trying to get the best faculty and the best staff on your campus, what do they need to see? What do they need to hear? What do they need to experience, to know that your institution is the best one for them? Because the one thing that a lot of colleges and universities have not figured out is that they are being interviewed just as much as they are interviewing potential candidates."

— Eddie Francis, brand strategy consultant/principal,
Edify Ventures, LLC, host of *I Wanna Work There!* podcast

Every job interview is an opportunity to start building that relationship, from the communications you send via email to the questions you ask during the interview. You are not only discovering if that person is the right fit for your institution, you are making sure the institution is the right fit for them.

"Think of it in terms of talent attraction, talent experience, and talent retention. Faculty and staff are the voice of the institution, so institutions must be intentional about who represents the brand voice. To attract talent, it's important to put in place content that prioritizes the brand so that every job candidate sees the kind of 'chorus' they will be singing in. For the best talent experience, content has to serve as a constant reminder of the brand voice that needs to be supported in their work. With that, the institution can retain the talent that benefits the institution—folks who represent the brand either directly or indirectly."

> — Eddie Francis, brand strategy consultant/principal,
> Edify Ventures, LLC, host of *I Wanna Work There!* podcast

Our employees can be our most vocal advocates or our most extreme critics. Make sure that your content and communications reflect the brand and consistently communicate the values and vision within the stories being shared.

"We tend to focus on external audiences. We sometimes forget we have these conversations internally on social media with our faculty and students. There are audiences out there that want to be part of the conversation. They have an interest and the ability to formulate a relationship, but they are just missing the boat because we are focused on other audiences, or focusing on one strategy when it comes to content marketing."

> — Karen Freberg, professor of strategic communication,
> University of Louisville, director, The Bird's Nest Student Agency

Do not overlook your internal audience. Creating content that helps them with professional development, sharing best practices, or connecting with resources can have a massive impact on their perception of their value within the institution.

Recognize your staff. Call them out when they have a win or do something particularly noteworthy. There are many things we can do with our content to help with retention.

"Having to constantly recruit new staff at all levels is going to end up being one of the biggest challenges higher education faces over the next 5 years."

> — Jeremy Tiers, senior director of admissions services,
> Tudor Collegiate Strategies

It is so difficult to get things done and focus on creating effective, quality content if you are spending your time doing someone else's work because they left for a better job. One of the best things you can do is to focus on employee retention, and one of the best ways to do that is to ensure they feel valued and recognized.

"To attract quality talent, however, it helps immensely to create an employer value proposition and content, such as employee testimonials, available on the careers microsite or webpage."

> — Eddie Francis, brand strategy consultant/principal,
> Edify Ventures, LLC, host of *I Wanna Work There!* podcast

Technology Changes

With the increasing use of generative AI, the changing Martech (marketing technology) landscape, and new content offerings in online and virtual environments, it is important that we continue to communicate with our internal audiences to let them know what resources we have available for them, what training there is, and how we are using these solutions to help make their lives easier.

There should be resources and content that help create transparency across your institutional landscape so people know what tools, training, and opportunities are being provided. It should not always be up to the employees to bring these things to leadership and request them.

Silos

Content marketing is the perfect solution to silos because it will not work in a vacuum. Effective content marketing requires collaboration, communication, and transparency.

"It can be a huge cultural shift to train staff to think that one story could have many different purposes and many different versions. I don't want one person to write the press release version, another person to write the social media content, and another person to write the story for the website. If you are a writer, you need to think about how the content can be used in different ways across different media, and you are likely going to create all those different versions. I want to put all people who develop content in any way, shape, or form together on a team. If that can't be done, at the bare minimum, we need a cross-functional group that meets at least once every week, reviewing what is coming in and what is going out this week. They need an editorial schedule where they're planning everything together and looking far out. A lot of it is about the planning, the tools, and the meeting together to talk through these things. Process, tools, and org structure are three of the key components."

> — Rachel Reuben Senor, vice president, account strategy,
> OHO Interactive

Once you start creating content that helps someone else's audience, they will immediately recognize the value of creating this shared content network. You will begin to recognize opportunities to reuse and leverage different pieces of content across multiple stories and for varied audiences.

"The thing that kills institutions is different groups all develop content strategies independently of each other, and they are focused on their individual needs. The content team becomes this production that meets the needs of each department but doesn't deliver value overall. Have proper content governance in place and an editorial board, or a place where all your silos meet regularly, to discuss content priorities as a unit. Then, the whole group of people who are responsible for content make a strategic decision about what the focus should be. This is a public content calendar, something you have all agreed on. It's such a simple hack, but I don't see it very often."

— Kyle Campbell, founder and managing director, Education Marketer

Establishing a network of communicators who meet regularly and share information is a huge step. However, people are already busy, and the last thing they want is another meeting in their schedule, so you have to look for ways to keep those meetings valuable and impactful.

Integrate an educational portion of the meeting so attendees walk away with actionable insights they can take away immediately. Create helpful resources or recommend other tools or processes you use that might be helpful to them.

"You need a really strong communicators network within an institution that meets on a regular basis. That creates the network you need for anyone across the institution that is creating content. If you're not in a centralized model, which most institutions aren't, you need to encourage deans or departments who are hiring people to hire writers. Writing is the most important skill set that someone needs in a decentralized staff member because then you can count on them to write content. The rest is either trainable or central can do it. The content writing is the heavy lift. Having people across campus creating content, then sharing our content, and we can share their content, and they are contributing to the essential content strategy; that is really the dream."

— Jamie Ceman, senior executive vice president, RW Jones Agency

While siloed teams are often opposed to the idea of centralization, once they see that it actually provides them with more resources, new skills, and increased ability to have their content promoted and shared, they quickly realize that it benefits everyone.

If the idea of centralization will keep people from working together, reframe it. Collaboration may be a more approachable term to use. It allows people to maintain their feeling of control while opening lines of communication to serve a greater purpose.

"Centralization should be important to every company out there. More often than not, several teams work on the same thing. Yet, our users see what they can. We are fighting for their attention like any other brand."

— Emanuel Díaz, head of content marketing, IE University

Once you start working across groups and teams that you have not worked with before, you will begin to see areas of crossover. Content that you can share and places where you can direct traffic to help promote their programs while they help you promote yours.

Stories do not happen in silos. They happen across multiple teams and areas within the institution.

"It's about aligning with your admissions team and understanding what is happening in real-time. Every college should have weekly or biweekly staff meetings where you have representation from admissions, marketing, financial aid, operations, athletics, and other key stakeholders."

— Jeremy Tiers, senior director of admissions services,
Tudor Collegiate Strategies

We do not understand other teams' audiences, strategies, or goals as well as they do. They can provide valuable insights to us on how to connect, what challenges they face, and what success looks like for them.

"Content marketing forces collaboration. The marketing and communications team can't develop a content strategy on their own. They have to be in lockstep with admissions to understand how this aligns with their cycle of admitting students. You have to understand how your content aligns with key dates and deadlines from the financial aid standpoint because it should support that work. It can be a tool to help marketing and comms teams build that collaboration and be that change agent to bring those disparate offices together, to look at how we're talking to people, what we're saying, when, and to whom."

— Carrie Phillips, chief communications and marketing officer,
University of Arkansas at Little Rock

Culture

Any change in a process, workflow, or strategy creates opportunities for other changes in our traditional models. If you are going to start implementing a centralized content marketing strategy, that is a great time to reassess things like chargeback processes, editorial calendar tools, and larger operations.

But what if you just want to start doing content marketing for your department or your team and you do not have the ability to start influencing changes in the larger institutional landscape? You can still be highly effective with content marketing on a smaller scale. That is the only way to start.

Content marketing is often about finding the "why" behind the story or content you need to create anyway. If someone brings a story idea to you, start by thinking about who the ideal audience is for that content. Who might be most helped or best served by the questions you can answer and the problems you can solve with that content? Then, how can you get that content consumer to do something that will help you make progress on one of your goals? Start there. Once you have those two things figured out, you can tell the story, answer the questions, solve the problems, and satisfy the person who brought you the idea.

"You may struggle with being led by the want or whim of powerful or important individuals in the institution, but we can serve that person's needs and university needs collectively. People are resistant to change unless the change serves their objectives better than what was done in the past."

— Tony Sheridan, senior digital campaigns manager,
KAUST (King Abdullah University of Science and Technology)

By bringing visibility to stories and creating content that features the impact of the values and mission of the institution, content marketing can help shape perceptions of our brand by showcasing certain aspects or integrations of our core beliefs in our communities and in society.

"Content marketing can take what an institution is known for, its climate, and the experiences of its community members and use these inputs to move, shape, expand, or tweak its culture. Marketing has a hard time generating culture, but it can shift, mold, and shape culture through content marketing and the reflection of stakeholder experiences."

— Teresa Valerio Parrot, EdD, APR, principal, TVP Communications, co-host of Trusted Voices podcast

EPIC THOUGHTS

- To address enrollment declines, use content marketing to improve retention of current students, promote in-demand programs to new audiences like adult learners, and showcase stories of how graduates' lives were transformed by their education beyond just career outcomes.

- Overcoming skepticism about the value of higher education requires telling authentic stories that allow audiences to see themselves in the experience and communicating the full benefits—not just knowledge or career outcomes but personal growth, learning to think critically, and becoming a better person.

- Faculty and staff are a critical but often overlooked audience for content marketing. Engaging them through content starting at recruitment and onboarding and continuing through their tenure is essential for attraction, experience, retention, and having them serve as effective brand ambassadors.

- Content marketing inherently breaks down silos by requiring cross-functional collaboration on audience insights, messages, and distribution. Establishing a strong communicators network and shared editorial calendar across the institution is key to integrated content marketing.

CHAPTER 7

Why Is Content Marketing So Difficult in Higher Education?

Launching a content marketing strategy can be difficult for any business. It is a mindset shift from what most marketing or communications teams are used to. No longer is it about just answering the five W and one H journalistic questions (who, what, when, where, why, and how); it is about really thinking audience first, audience-centric, and connecting that to your goals and values.

It is about answering different and deeper questions like, "Who cares? Why do they care? What do they need? How can we help?"

It is about saying no to content that does not support the strategy and figuring out the best perspective on the content that does. It is about changing our workflow from one focused on putting out a specific volume of content to one focused on creating media that can tell our stories in multiple ways.

This can be even more difficult in higher education, partially due to our resistance to change and our deep-seated cultural issues, but also because it is such a shift from the way we have always done things. It is very easy to start to slip back into our conditioned patterns.

"Too many times, we try to promote the institution and focus on the features of the institution, as opposed to recognizing the benefits that the students and influencers (i.e., moms) want to know. I think we miss the opportunity with content marketing because people think, 'Oh, we're just going to have the faculty write a blog.' Well, no, that doesn't answer the questions. It's simply just another place for us to beat our chests and say, 'Look how smart we are.' It's a different mindset that academia needs to get into."

— Bart Caylor, president and founder, Caylor Solutions,
president, The Higher Ed Marketer, author of *Chasing Mission Fit*

Coming up with a codified and specific content marketing strategy and mission statement will not only help you keep your team on track; it will help you communicate your changing workflow to other groups across the institution.

Most importantly, it will give you something to present to stakeholders who come with requests for certain pieces of content featuring particular elements. A documented strategy, especially once you have data to back up its effectiveness, will give you the ability to say, "That story or piece of content does not fit into our new content marketing strategy."

Of course, it is a good idea to have alternative solutions in mind for those requests. Maybe that piece of content works better as a social post or within a department newsletter. There is probably some way to distribute it, but not within the new strategy.

"Higher education institutions have many stakeholders who feel like they have a right to review and amend and criticize the content. Occasionally, they'll praise, but mostly, they criticize. Managing that bewildering array of internal stakeholders is the first major issue for content marketing. Second is getting and maintaining a level of investment to make content marketing worthwhile. In so many institutions, somebody gets excited and says, 'In the first year, we're going to do this really cool marketing thing, we're going to do this really cool content thing.' And they might invest a lot in the beginning. Then it becomes background noise. So, the ability of colleges and universities to support this as the kind of sustained investment one needs to make marketing effective is a real weakness in the system. The third part is the failure to invest adequately in a strategy or approach. There's this intriguing counter-relationship between marketing and prestige. If you are deemed to be prestigious, you're also believed not to need marketing. That's a very difficult thing to push back on."

> — Michael Schoenfeld, partner, global co-lead for foundations,
> education, and global health sector, Brunswick Group

Many higher education leaders expect to see immediate and measurable results from marketing efforts. That is what they are used to.

Setting expectations early and getting leadership buy-in to this strategy is critical to its success. The number one reason that most content marketing strategies fail is because they are not given enough time to work.

Building trust and creating relationships is not a quick process.

"If I think about our comms flows pre–content marketing, it was just calls to action. Visit, apply, visit, apply, here is what you should know about, visit, apply, visit, apply. There was no sticky content. There was no content that was relevant and timely to the end user that wasn't just selling. I think that was a mind shift for the admissions team who wanted them to inquire and apply. We said, 'We're going to get them there, but it's not a straight line. They're going to wiggle around in this journey. How do we consistently stay in front of them and stay a relevant source for them?'"

> — Angela Polec, vice president for strategic marketing and
> communications, Temple University

What Is a Brand, and What Creates It?

"Your brand is what other people say about you when you're not in the room."

> — Steve Jobs

Apple is certainly one of the most iconic brands around. B2B and B2C businesses spend lots of time, money, and resources building their brand, establishing their identity, and then consistently focusing their messaging, marketing, and promotions around the brand.

The brand, as a concept, is often challenging to many higher education institutions because it can be difficult to create and maintain a brand that stands out, for several reasons. One of the issues is that there are so many other institutions with similar curricula and missions. Another is that leadership can change in higher education, and the new leader may have different ideas of what that brand should be and what the goals and values are of an institution.

"Everybody knows the word *brand*, and everybody wants a new brand. Everybody is just rebranding. But people need to understand the core brand, which shouldn't be changing.

Maybe you refresh every four or five years, but we should not constantly be looking to rebrand. Your brand is the equity that you have in the market. It's the creative execution that you refresh from time to time. But people love rebrands. New presidents love rebrands."

— Jamie Ceman, senior executive vice president, RW Jones Agency

While brands can evolve and change to reflect issues in society, the fundamental brand of an institution should remain consistent. When changes to the foundational brand are announced, it can cause confusion, consternation, and anger from your audiences who have a specific vision in their head of what the institution stands for.

You can change the priorities, implementation, and focus of your brand values to support new initiatives and address changing issues, but you should always look to do that while ensuring that your underlying brand tenets are still supported.

"I believe that content has always been important, yet what matters to people has evolved. Now, we are driven by the purpose and the values of the brands we follow. Students care about what their institutions are doing about gender, sustainability, poverty, accessibility, and so many more things. As any other brand, we should take a stand about these things because we owe it to the new generations to make an impact in the world."

> — Emanuel Díaz, head of content marketing, IE University

A key element of your content should be brand alignment. If you start putting out content or stories that do not match up with what you claim as your brand values, your audiences will recognize that quickly.

The messages and the content that goes out to your audiences need to be clearly aligned with your brand.

"In terms of content marketing, you have to know what to tell folks. A big part of that is to find ways to articulate your brand voice, especially in terms of mission, vision, and core values. People want to know what the institution values, and core values are a guide for how people behave and how they make decisions. I keep screaming from the mountaintops, 'Gen Z—they are your new employees.' They are not going to sit around and listen to an administrator say, 'I'm all about people,' and then that same administrator says, 'Yeah, we don't care how many people we lose, we're going to replace them—no problem.'"

> — Eddie Francis, brand strategy consultant/principal,
> Edify Ventures, LLC, host of *I Wanna Work There!* podcast

Promoting and circulating brand messaging is as important for internal audiences as it is for external audiences. Embodying the brand is more than just a checkbox as part of an annual review process.

It is about taking action and doing your work in a way that intentionally supports the institutional brand. It is about how you act, how you relate and communicate with others, and how you think about what you are doing.

"Your people are your brand, not some tagline that's in your marketing materials. What are people saying about you, your colleagues, and your students when you are not around?"

> — Jeremy Tiers, senior director of admissions services,
> Tudor Collegiate Strategies

Your brand messages are what will stick with people when they start to know and remember you. That awareness will often come from the content they consume. This is why it is critical that the content is not only valuable and helpful for that audience, but that it supports your brand mission and architecture.

"It starts with your brand. Every message that comes out of the university should roll up to your brand, because that's how you ensure that no matter who is looking at what, they will remember the same underlying core."

> — Dayana Kibilds, strategist, Ologie, speaker, co-author of *Mailed It: A Guide to Crafting Emails That Build Relationships and Get Results*, host of Enrollify's *Talking Tactics* podcast

Differentiate Your Brand

Differentiation can be difficult in higher education because, fundamentally, all higher education institutions have a similar purpose: to educate their students. If you stop there, there is no differentiation. But we do not stop there.

To truly differentiate, you must be focused, niche down to select a smaller audience segment and decide what to prioritize.

What can your institution do better than any other institution out there? What is it that makes you different? Your curricula? Your faculty? Your students? What is it that makes a particular type of student connect with you in a way they do not connect with any other institution?

"We have a powerful story to tell. Every university, every higher ed institution does. Knowing who you are, and what stories are most strategic to tell, is important because you don't have unlimited bandwidth within your intended audiences. You can't tell them 72 things about yourself and think that they will remember and visualize you as that. Avoiding brand fragmentation in your content marketing is incredibly important. You can't be a center of excellence of 72 different things."

> — Tony Sheridan, senior digital campaigns manager, KAUST (King Abdullah University of Science and Technology)

Once you establish your brand and figure out what it is that truly differentiates you, you have what you need to target your most desirable audience. Once you have your brand differentiation figured out, you know what it is that will make you succeed and be an essential part of the higher education landscape.

"The number one thing any of us have to do is to protect the brands of our institution and be thoughtful about that. But if we can keep helping people understand what we do, and build respect for it and appreciation of it, hopefully, that starts building some benefits when questions come up on these more challenging issues."

> — Paul Rand, vice president of communications, University of Chicago, host of *Big Brains* podcast

Your content cannot just be the same content you see from everyone else. It has to be stories and messages that you are uniquely positioned to tell. It needs to be advice, answers, and solutions that you have the expertise and authority to speak on. Then you have to put it out where your audience will find it.

"I look at content as a way to extend the surface area of your brand around a given topic. Content marketing can be highly effective if your goal will be furthered, but it's also about resourcing and sustainability. It is a valuable tactic when it's done with purpose. It's more than just what you create. It's the system in which it's placed. Is it optimized to be discovered? Is it then optimized to pull people in and convert them and bring them into some kind of flow? Is it written with distinction? Are we finding a way to leverage our knowledge product that reflects what is special about our institution?"

> — Georgy Cohen, director of digital strategy, OHO Interactive

Consistency and Commitment

Consistency is one of the six principles of a successful content marketing strategy. In the words of Joe Pulizzi, "To be great, you have to show up. Then you have to be interesting. *Every. Single. Time.*"

Consistency is not only about how often you put out content, it is about the *quality* of the content you put out.

"Leaning into that combination of audience and creativity is the foundation for effective content marketing."

> — Tim Jones, director, brand and integrated strategy,
> SimpsonScarborough

Another principle of content marketing is to be the best of breed. Every time you put out content, try to make it the most impactful, relevant, engaging, and entertaining content you can. Do not wait until the day before your content is supposed to be delivered and then throw something together. You need to do the research and you need to do the work. Understand what your audience wants and make your best effort to overdeliver.

"The fallacy of content marketing is you can't just stop it. You can't send one thing out and be like, 'It didn't work.' There will be a premium on that idea of creatively going back to that audience again and again. That is going to be a compelling challenge for many institutions."

> — Tim Jones, director, brand and integrated strategy,
> SimpsonScarborough

EPIC THOUGHTS

- Shifting to an audience-centric mindset focused on providing value versus just promoting the institution is challenging. Having a documented content marketing strategy and leadership buy-in is critical to stay on track and manage stakeholder requests that do not align.

- Building and maintaining a differentiated higher education brand is difficult with so many institutions having similar missions. Content marketing can help by consistently showcasing the institution's unique expertise, experiences, and values that make it stand out to specific audiences.

- Institutions often struggle to sustain the level of investment needed to make content marketing effective long-term. Setting expectations up front that building trusted relationships through content is a gradual process is key to maintaining leadership support.

CHAPTER 8

Case Studies

Purdue University: Transforming Higher Education Marketing Through Authentic Storytelling

"They started with the strategic plan of the university and by focusing on the five strategic initiatives, or focus areas, to pursue over the next decade. Then they translated that into a brand strategy by asking, 'What are the timeless messages? What do we stand for? What are we about, at the end of the day? How do we want people to think of us in an evergreen way? What are the key pillars that we should organize our content around?' Basically, a value proposition and messaging strategy for the overall university. Then they translated that into a content strategy. And it's curated. They don't throw everything out there; they identify the things they feel most represent that strategy, then they repeat, and repeat, and repeat, and they find ways to make it interesting."

— Bill Faust, president, Ologie

Purdue University has emerged as a leading example of effective content marketing in higher education. They have won numerous awards and have been recognized for their work in many ways, including being the only university on Fast Company's Brands That Matter list three years in a row. By focusing on authentic, emotionally resonant storytelling, Purdue has built powerful connections with its audiences and achieved unprecedented levels of engagement.

Shifting from Order-Takers to Strategic Storytellers

In 2018, the marketing landscape at Purdue was fragmented and tactical. A fundamental shift in mindset and structure was essential to Purdue's marketing transformation. Kelly Hiller, vice president of marketing at Purdue, explains, "The first step was the budgeting process, and making sure that we could structure our budget in a way that we were no longer beholden to the recharge, and that we weren't relying on other units around campus to hire us to fulfill their orders."

This change empowered Purdue's marketing team to focus on strategic, audience-centric content, rather than simply taking orders -- but it also required additional staffing and resources. Hiller notes, "When you're no longer order takers and are drivers of great marketing, that requires some additional talent. When we started this, we were a team of about 55. Now we're bumping on 100."

To continue being a good partner, they created, and regularly update, a library of content packages for their campus partners to provide access to resources and assets they can use for their projects and channels. Every package includes information on usage, links, social best practices, and much more to help other teams leverage the content effectively.

When discussing the approach, Hiller adds, "We view it as a team effort. A big change for us in mindset was our 150th anniversary. That was a university-wide effort I had never seen in my 18 years here. I had never witnessed such coordination. And people got used to it, they saw the benefits of singing the same song and amplifying content together and what that looks like. We all want that."

Hiller has seen this shift create more opportunities to work with other teams across the university, saying, "It has fostered a scenario where they see the value of us all working together and pushing things out together, and the value of that amplification. We have a greater level of coordination and conversation with people pitching us ideas on things we should do and put out. A lot of times, they are great ideas and things that we want to pursue. At the end of the day, it's a win-win for everybody."

Ali McNichols, director of brand content at Purdue, expands on this, saying, "When we reach out to our campus partners at the beginning of a story about them, we ask 'Who should we talk to? What's the best angle for this? This is what we're thinking, do you agree with it?' They have the connections and the relationships. You don't always get the opportunity to work together when you're in colleges and central units, so that's nice. Then, once you get it out in the world, they are sharing it on their channels, which works even better for affinity because they have a really strong connection with their alumni who are extremely loyal to the college from which they graduated."

Every month, the Purdue Communicators Council comes together. This group has more than 500 communicators and marketers across the spectrum of experience, role, and team size. These meetings are a mix of updates, the latest content, and featured resources as well as training and education in breakout sessions.

"I learn from my colleagues every day," says McNichols, "And I am very blessed to be surrounded by very talented people. The best way to learn is by doing, and this work truly is case study after case study of marketing expertise. So many cool things that you just can't teach in a classroom, you have to experience it."

Building Cross-Functional Teams Around Content

To support this new strategic focus, Purdue restructured its marketing department into cross-functional teams dedicated to specific content types or audiences.

This structure facilitates close collaboration and keeps everyone committed to crafting resonant content. "It gives people the structure, the team, and the momentum to do bigger things together," says Emily Richwine, senior creative director. "Each team is focused on a different area. Right now, we have a team working on admissions. We have another team we call Storymakers that is telling more of those deep, connected, emotive stories. Each team has everyone it needs to tell a great story: a strategist, a project manager, a writer, a designer, a videographer, a photographer, social media experts, so each team runs as its own little mini agency—super nimble and super powerful."

Authentic Storytelling That Connects Emotionally

At the core of Purdue's content strategy lies a commitment to authentic, emotionally compelling storytelling that showcases real student and alumni experiences. Richwine states, "I'm so inspired by our students. The two big spots we have done recently, 'What Can You Imagine at Purdue' and the sequel, 'What Comes Next?,' were inspired by real students, their real dreams. They say things like, 'I'm going to go to Mars.' And I truly believe them. Their dreams are the most inspiring thing in the world."

This approach has resonated with audiences. Hiller recounts the impact of their breakout "What Can You Imagine at Purdue" video, "I had the privilege of speaking at the Purdue Women's Conference, and there were a couple of women of color in the audience, and they were brought to tears because they're like, 'That's me, and I've never seen myself portrayed that way before. It's like you brought my story to life.'"

Emphasizing the importance of understanding and targeting specific audiences, McNichols says, "At the end of the day, the thing that I talk about the most with our team is that people are savvy. It's 2024. The world is very advanced. Marketing initiatives and technologies are very advanced. There are so many things that we know and can learn about our audiences. It's just being smart about your marketing and figuring out what you need to know about those audiences to craft that content to them."

Empowering Student Creators
Through Boiler Ambassadors

Purdue directly involves students in content creation through its innovative "Boiler Ambassadors" program. These ambassadors are often featured within institutional content, and they produce authentic peer-to-peer content themselves.

"They have their own Instagram channel," says Richwine. "It's called @boilerambassadors, and they create all their own content. They also help us with reels, ideas, and trends. We have had the students do welcome videos for us or admissions content because they know what prospective students want to see—and they are way cooler than we're going to be."

By empowering students to share their own stories, Purdue ensures its content remains relevant and relatable to prospective students.

Key Takeaways

- Align your content strategy with institutional brand and values. As Hiller emphasizes, it is crucial to "be making sure that we are aligning with the attitudes, beliefs, and behaviors that we are looking to influence and strengthen with our brand."

- Invest in audience research to craft resonant content. "We invest a lot of time in learning about our audiences," states McNichols. "We do a lot of data analysis and research trying to understand our audiences. We spend a lot of time doing performance analysis. If something's not working, we'll change it. We will switch something up and try something different. Knowing about our audience better allows us to craft stories they are looking for, that will help convert them. And not only convert, but build brand affinity, which is something that we really care about."

- Structure teams for collaboration and focus. Purdue's cross-functional teams allow for specialized expertise while maintaining cohesive storytelling. Richwine explains that team members "have their work team, and then they have their home base of other creatives just like them." While the work teams talk about their specific projects, each week the different creative teams (writers, videographers, designers, etc.) will meet to talk about other opportunities.

- Prioritize authentic stories that showcase student experiences.

- Involve students directly in content creation. Through programs like Boiler Ambassadors, Purdue empowers students to create content that connects with other students and potential students. "I think just listening to them talk is so powerful. They are a constant inspiration," shares Richwine.

By shifting away from an order-taking mindset and embracing authentic storytelling, investing in audience understanding, and amplifying student voices, Purdue has set a new standard for content marketing in higher education.

Redefining their team structure, increasing collaboration across the institution, and involving students in the content process has led not only to increased engagement but also to distinct brand awareness that stands out in the higher education landscape.

University of Chicago: Harnessing the Power of Podcasting in Higher Education Marketing

Public confidence in the value of a university degree and academic research is eroding. Combating these perceptions requires universities to reengage with their key stakeholders in authentic and impactful ways. Increasingly, forward-thinking institutions are turning to content marketing to showcase their groundbreaking research and ideas.

The University of Chicago has been at the vanguard of this movement with its pioneering Big Brains podcast and podcast network. Launched in 2019, Big Brains provides a platform for world-class scholars to share their pathbreaking research and insights with a broad audience. In doing so, it is helping control the narrative around higher education's value proposition. As Paul M. Rand, the University of Chicago's vice president of communications, explains:

"Ten years ago, you had 90 plus percent of all parents in this country wanting their children to go to college. This number is in the mid-40s right now. You're seeing a great push and resistance against higher education, against university research. If we can help our faculty showcase their work in a way that is engaging, and explains it in a timely, thoughtful basis, so that a large group of people can understand, we thought there could be an audience for that. That's where the initial idea for Big Brains came from."

Bringing Complex Ideas to Life

At the heart of Big Brains' success is its ability to translate complex academic ideas into accessible and engaging content. Each episode features an in-depth conversation with a leading scholar, delving into their research and its real-world implications. But rather than getting bogged down in jargon or minutiae, the show focuses on storytelling and the human dimensions of scholarly work. Rand elaborates:

"I [was] here at the University of Chicago as the head of communications and truly every day I met somebody just utterly remarkable. Not only were they extraordinary in what they were studying and what their research was, but almost overwhelmingly they were just really lovely people. I found that I was having great conversations with them, and I thought, what a great idea to have a podcast; to treat it almost as a dinner conversation with somebody whose life's work we are going to get a chance to explore."

This approach has struck a chord with audiences, who tune in by the thousands to hear experts talk about everything from the science of empathy to the economics of crime. Some of the most popular episodes have explored topical issues like the importance of early childhood education, the root causes of violence, and the psychology of political polarization. By tackling social issues through the lens of academic research, Big Brains can add nuance and depth to the public discourse.

Building a Loyal Following

Since launching in 2019, Big Brains has grown into one of higher education's most successful podcasts, with episodes regularly getting between 8,000 and 15,000 listens and thousands more YouTube views and transcript readings. But its impact extends beyond just the numbers. The show has become a focal point for intellectual life at the University of Chicago, sparking conversations across campus and beyond. It has helped to build affinity with key stakeholders like prospective students, alumni, and donors. As Rand notes:

"Impact comes in many forms. We know some of our scholars have created new partnerships and received funding from people learning about their work. People around the world and at different institutions are writing and saying they would like to be featured on the show, and even people who come to the institution because they heard the podcast and want to be in rooms with people like that."

Big Brains is not a one-off effort, but part of a holistic content strategy. The university has launched an entire podcast network, with multiple shows catering to niche audiences like policymakers and business leaders. It has also developed a range of supporting content, from episode transcripts and show notes to social media assets and newsletter features. By meeting audiences where they are and providing multiple avenues for engagement, the University of Chicago can maximize the impact and reach of its thought leadership.

An Investment in the Future

None of this success happened overnight. Launching and sustaining a high-quality podcast requires a significant investment of time, talent, and resources. Big Brains has a dedicated team of producers, researchers, and marketers who work to develop compelling content and grow the show's audience. As Rand cautions:

"It's not cheap and it's not easy. It's not for the quick hit. We have a team of people who work on it. We have folks who help us produce, help us research the topics on the different shows, are editors, and help craft a storyline."

But for the University of Chicago, this long-term orientation is a bonus. By taking a strategic approach to podcasting, the university has built a sustainable platform for thought leadership that advances its overarching institutional mission.

Key Takeaways

The Big Brains podcast offers a compelling case study of the power of content marketing for higher education. By leveraging its intellectual capital to create authentic and impactful content, the University of Chicago can engage with key audiences, establish itself as a thought leader, and advance its strategic objectives. Here are some of the key takeaways:

- Identify your unique value proposition. Every university has a wealth of intellectual capital in the form of its faculty, researchers, staff, and students. Podcasting provides an ideal format to showcase their expertise and bring their ideas to life for a broad audience.

- Take a long-term approach. Building a successful podcast requires a sustained investment of time and resources. Focus on telling compelling stories and delivering value to your audience, rather than chasing quick wins or vanity metrics.

- Integrate podcasting into a holistic content strategy. Maximize the impact of your podcast by developing ancillary content that can be repurposed across owned, earned, and paid channels.

- Align your efforts with your institutional mission. Ultimately, podcasting should serve to advance your university's overarching strategic objectives. Use it as a tool to build affinity, combat misperceptions, and demonstrate your institution's value to society.

By following these principles, higher education marketers can harness the power of podcasting to cut through the noise, engage with key stakeholders, and build lasting relationships that advance their institutional goals. As the University of Chicago has demonstrated, the institutions that prioritize authentic and impactful content will be best positioned to thrive in an increasingly competitive and scrutinized higher education landscape.

Michigan State University's Impactful "Spartans Will" Campaign: Engaging Audiences Through Strategic Content

In the complex landscape of higher education, institutions are tasked with engaging a diverse range of audiences, including prospective and current students, alumni, faculty, staff, and the wider community.

Each audience requires tailored messaging and content to effectively communicate the university's brand, values, and offerings. Michigan State University (MSU) has tackled this challenge head-on through its "Spartans Will" campaign, demonstrating the crucial role of content marketing in driving institutional goals.

Through comprehensive research, a compelling brand platform, and strategic content distribution, MSU has cultivated deep connections with its audiences and strengthened its reputation with a strategy that has endured for more than 14 years amidst challenges, scandals, and several leadership changes.

Building the Foundation

Launched in 2010, the "Spartans Will" campaign was rooted in extensive research conducted with Simpson Scarborough to understand perceptions across stakeholder groups. Heather Swain, vice president for marketing, public relations and digital strategy, noted the importance of this groundwork:

"We started with research, where all good work should start. Doing comprehensive research across a broad number of audiences and stakeholders, internal and external, trying to figure out what the perceptions were and what the gap was between what we thought they should be. A key insight emerged when asking audiences about positioning statements that fit the university today versus their projections for five years in the future," Swain explained. "They were all over the place for today, but five years out they coalesced toward something that gave us a map we could work with to build and articulate a brand."

This foundation allowed MSU to craft a brand platform that not only encapsulated the land-grant mission but also carved out a distinct position. Over time, they have refined the platform to dive deeper into what makes MSU unique.

Activating "Spartans Will"

The "Spartans Will" tagline, developed by MSU's agency partner, 160over90, initially sparked mixed reactions due to its dual meaning.

However, it has shown remarkable longevity and adoption over the past 14 years. Swain reflected:

"It was not an overnight hit. Some people were a little troubled by the dual meaning. Others loved it. But it has grown to be adopted and held by our community, even more tightly than I could have imagined."

MSU has capitalized on both aspects of the tagline—the inherent determination and resilience of Spartans, and a call to action around the impact Spartans make in the world. This messaging has permeated content across channels, from brand advertising to storytelling around students, faculty, and alumni.

Swain shared a pivotal moment: "We broke our brand standards and decoupled our plume from the rest of the helmet and then put it over people. That allowed a symbol to cross the line from athletics into the rest of the university. Then it became everybody's symbol, and the tagline became everybody's tagline, too."

Perhaps most surprisingly, the "Spartans Will" campaign endured a significant reputational crisis at MSU. Swain remarked, "It surprised me that it survived, I did not expect that. I expected to sunset it. However, research showed that key audiences separated the Spartan identity from the institution's failings. Alumni in particular felt ready to stand back up and reclaim their Spartan identity," said Swain. "And when tested directly, our research clearly showed a preference for continuing to use Spartans Will moving forward."

A Strategic Content Framework

To effectively engage audiences through content, MSU has developed a framework that maps to its brand platform while also supporting organizational reputation and trust-building efforts. Swain outlined their approach:

"We have built a statistically validated model for alumni around affinity and the factors that drive it. We know that perception of excellence is one pathway, but [so is] community. To trust an organization, you need to know they're going in the right direction, so we have content that we are constantly thinking about and working on to build into each one of those things."

This framework guides content creation and distribution, ensuring messaging ladders up to overarching goals. For example, knowing that belief in leadership contributes to overall trust, MSU develops content to showcase its leaders and decision-making.

The Vital Role of Content Marketing

When asked about the importance of content marketing in higher education, Swain unequivocally stated, "It's vital. It's how you activate every channel. It's how you can make intellectual arguments, and it's really the only way to get that emotional connection."

She sees significant potential for universities to better understand audiences and deliver the right content at key moments:

"We create an enormous amount of content. What we can do better is ratchet down, not create so much, and learn more about our audiences and what those moments are when they truly need or want that content, and [then] create what can serve and connect with them better."

At MSU, this has looked like mapping content to the prospective student journey and developing content to address key questions at each stage. They are also investing in personalization and segmentation to move beyond a "publisher mode" of just pushing out information into a more reciprocal relationship.

Measuring Impact

To gauge the performance of their content marketing efforts, MSU is working to tag content either directly within platforms or during analysis of aggregate channel data. Swain noted that this tagging taxonomy is essential for efficient and meaningful measurement.

By understanding which messages and stories are resonating with key audiences, MSU can continually optimize its content strategy. This data-driven approach ensures resources are allocated to the most impactful initiatives.

Key Takeaways

- Start with comprehensive audience research to understand perceptions, identify gaps, and craft a differentiated brand platform that can guide content strategy over the long term.

- Develop a compelling, flexible tagline and visual identity that can be adopted widely across the university to unite athletics and academics under a shared brand.

- Create a strategic content framework mapped to the brand platform and key reputation/trust-building goals, ensuring content ladders up to overarching objectives.

- Invest in understanding audience needs and journeys to deliver the right content at key moments, moving beyond just pushing out information to building reciprocal relationships.

- Implement a taxonomy for tagging and measuring content performance within platforms to enable ongoing optimization of the content strategy based on what resonates with priority audiences.

Michigan State University's "Spartans Will" campaign offers a compelling case study on the power of brand-aligned content marketing in higher education. By investing in audience research, crafting a differentiated brand platform, and developing a strategic framework for content creation and distribution, MSU has fostered deep connections with its constituents.

As Swain reflected, content is truly the only way to achieve emotional resonance and engagement at scale. For higher education marketers seeking to make an impact, the lessons are clear: understand your audiences, deliver content that both meets their needs and ladders up to institutional goals, and measure performance to enable ongoing optimization.

In a crowded and competitive landscape, content marketing is essential for universities to cut through the noise, convey their unique value proposition, and build lasting relationships. MSU's success with

"Spartans Will" demonstrates that with a strategic, audience-centric approach, institutions can harness the full potential of content to drive reputation, affinity, and organizational success.

Bringing Harvard into Focus: How Content Marketing Transformed the University's Homepage and Engagement

The Challenge

Harvard University, one of the most prestigious institutions in the world, found itself grappling with a common problem in higher education: how to effectively leverage its homepage to engage a variety of key audiences. The existing homepage was outdated, cluttered, and failed to resonate with most visitors. Aaron Baker, senior associate director of content strategy, candidly admitted, "Nobody at Harvard cared about the homepage."

Compounding the issue was the fact that Harvard's homepage audience was vastly different from that of other higher education institutions. "The Harvard homepage is unique because so much traffic comes from people who are completely unaffiliated," said Melissa Lesica, director of content strategy. "It didn't make sense. Why would these people be coming if they aren't interested in being students, they're not alumni, there's nothing tying them to the organization?"

Further analysis revealed that the homepage was operating more like a news site than a traditional .edu site. Lesica noted, "What we found was that they were coming for information, to become more aware or knowledgeable about a specific topic. That made all of us on the team reconsider what we were building."

The Solution

Recognizing the need for a bold new approach, Baker and Lesica proposed a complete overhaul of the Harvard homepage centered around content strategy principles. The goal was to create a dynamic editorial product that would "inspire, educate, and engage users" while showcasing Harvard's world-class expertise and research.

To inform the new strategy, the team conducted extensive user research, competitive analysis, stakeholder interviews, and more. "The research was super important, not only for us to understand what people use the site for, but also to sell it to leadership," explained Lesica. "Having this foundation of research to draw from and to pin all of their questions back to data and focus groups and surveys—it was critical in selling it to leadership because it is a completely different concept than what anyone else was doing."

The resulting "In Focus" approach features topical content takeovers that dive deep into a single issue, such as artificial intelligence, climate change, arts and culture, and more. By curating content from across Harvard's many schools and departments, In Focus allows the institution's incredible breadth and depth of knowledge to shine.

To bring In Focus to life, the team established an intentional editorial process complete with brainstorming sessions, cross-departmental content planning meetings, and an internal newsletter to socialize upcoming topics and solicit content from across the university.

"Opening up to the entire university brought our partners into our process," explained Lesica. "Then they could either create new content or dig up previous content, which made our jobs so much easier. This process is great for our audience, but it's also great for our employees who were able to be content strategists and think, 'What is the best piece of content? How does it work? What headings are we going to use? What does our editorial calendar look like?'"

Baker adds, "We let them be the subject matter experts and they tell us who to talk to."

The In Focus concept was socialized and sold in from the ground up, rather than handed down from leadership as a mandate. "It was boots on the ground," said Lesica. "It was people who update their social media, who update their homepages, who are going through the same process. We wanted to hear that they were buying into this concept so that we knew we could execute successfully."

The Results

The impact of In Focus on Harvard's homepage and overall digital presence has been nothing short of transformative. Engagement metrics like page views, scroll depth, and time on site have significantly improved. The topical focus has also bolstered Harvard's SEO performance, with In Focus pages serving as powerful pillar pages to establish authority and rankings around key topics.

Perhaps even more importantly, In Focus has sparked a cultural shift toward greater collaboration, transparency, and editorial-style thinking across the university. "The cycle of improved data for all people and more eyeballs on your content has become a self-fulfilling prophecy of creating better content for the homepage," said Lesica.

Even in decentralized higher education environments, content can be a powerful unifying force. "I think it's really important, especially because we are so decentralized, that there is this one area that everyone knows the plan going forward," said Lesica. "We try to be as open as possible when things do shift. We try to explain why they did. And there is at least one place where everyone can be on the same page."

Key Takeaways

The Harvard In Focus case study offers several crucial content marketing lessons for higher education institutions of all sizes:

- Start with your audience. Let user research and data, not internal assumptions, drive your content strategy.

- Embrace an editorial mindset. Treat your homepage and key content properties as storytelling vehicles, not just marketing real estate.

- Go narrow and deep. Use content pillars to establish authority and engagement around key topics that resonate with your audiences.

- Democratize content planning. Socialize your strategy, build relationships, and create avenues for communicators across the institution to participate.

- Lead with data and research. Ground your content strategy in user insights and clear KPIs to earn leadership buy-in and ongoing support.

- Think holistically about content governance. Use taxonomies, templates, and publishing workflows to ensure content quality and consistency at scale.

Looking ahead, the worlds of higher education and content marketing will continue to evolve at a breakneck pace. By staying grounded in audience needs, building cross-functional relationships, and adapting strategically to new channels and technologies, university communications teams can navigate the chaos and keep their institutions relevant and resonant.

With the right strategy and mindset, content can be a transformative force in higher education—inspiring audiences, showcasing expertise, and forging connections across even the most complex institutions.

CHAPTER 9

How to Create Epic Content Marketing

So, we have talked about what content marketing is and how you can use it in higher education. We have looked at some excellent case studies of epic content marketing. But how do you actually execute this? What are some actionable steps you can take to launch a content marketing strategy and then create your epic content?

Let's walk through some initial steps and workflow that will help you create and manage a successful content marketing strategy.

"The content is already there. We are so fortunate because universities are a gold mine of content. There is innovation happening. There is teaching happening. Students are accomplishing things. Professors are making breakthroughs. There is so much content at your university that, when you're thinking about creating a content marketing strategy, it's not about what content you need to create; it's about what processes and workflows you need so the stories can actually get to you."

— Dayana Kibilds, strategist, Ologie, speaker, co-author of *Mailed It: A Guide to Crafting Emails That Build Relationships and Get Results*, host of Enrollify's *Talking Tactics* podcast

Before you can come up with your content marketing strategy, you will need to clearly understand the institutional strategy, school strategy, department strategies, and whatever else your content marketing strategy will need to support. You will also need to clearly define the primary audience that you are going to target.

"The real work of drilling down to set meaningful objectives and goals often has not been done. It's only when we do that work that you can actually make any of this measurable, so it's an important first step. The second piece is audience research. We have a structure we use to think about our audiences. There are four things that you need to know about your audiences to do content marketing or any content strategy. The access layer: what channels and platforms they use. The information management layer: what are the information leads they have. The third layer looks at motivations and values; the things that make our hearts beat as human beings, the things that set us apart individually, and the things that are going to make the difference between whether we want to jump out of bed in the morning or not. The last piece is the influences and the distractions. It's only when you know those four layers that you are able to do content marketing."

> — Tracy Playle, chief content strategist, Pickle Jar Communications,
> author of *The Connected Campus*

There are several things you will need to have in place to establish the framework you will need to reach your goals. You will need certain skill sets within your team. You will need a solid understanding of what you are planning to do, why you are going to do it, and how you are going to accomplish it.

"There's too much to get your arms around all at once. The key is creating a responsible group of people. In a small institution, that might be one person; in a bigger institution, it might be hundreds of people. Create a team that is responsible, [that] has a charter around the alignment and coordination of communication. It's not an on-demand vending machine of content but is a leading organization that is meant to create the standards, the operational approaches, the playbooks, and the ways that the institution will speak. Whether that's messaging architectures, persona development, audience development, and alignment of content-oriented tools. One of the simplest things that we have seen done by larger organizations is to just get alignment on nomenclature.

What is a campaign? What is an initiative? What is marketing? What is an e-book? What is a blog post? What is an article? What is a white paper? Even identifying and getting to a common definition of those things can move the needle in a huge way."

> — Robert Rose, chief strategy officer, The Content Advisory,
>   chief strategy advisor, Content Marketing Institute, author,
>   co-host of *This Old Marketing* podcast

Once you have done the research, you will need to be sure you have someone to create the content and tell the stories. This does not have to be a dedicated person (although it is great if you have those kinds of resources) but it does need to be someone who understands the fundamentals of storytelling.

"Storytelling is a skill. The first step is to recognize that you need skills to fill that gap. A lot of universities don't have it because they do not think like publishers to begin with. They're not used to thinking like journalists, and they don't understand that there is this gap between taking a student's testimonial and figuring out what the hooks are and presenting it for different audiences in different formats. It goes beyond the skill set of a content creator, social media professional, or marketing officer."

> — Kyle Campbell, founder and managing director, Education Marketer

Creating the content and stories does not necessarily require an incredible writer, depending on what your primary delivery platform is going to be, but, even if you are creating videos, most of those start with some sort of script or content outline. Thus, writing skills will be essential.

Do Your Content Research

Before you start creating more content and figuring out which stories you are going to tell, it is important to know what content you already have. The best way to do that is to start with an audit.

Figure out what types of content are already being created, who is creating it, what the audiences are (if they are defined), and where the gaps might be.

If you know you are going to begin with a particular target audience, find out what content is already being delivered to them, how frequently, and what topics are typically being covered.

"An audit is a good place to start. That can be done by an outside firm or with an internal team by sampling communications. Start by creating a secret shopper operation for different audience segments so you can see everything that folks receive. New York University decided to create a ghost prospective student account just to see what students were receiving between the points of an admission offer and their enrollment in the first couple of weeks at the institution. It gave them the opportunity to understand the frequency, the nature of the content, and the senders of the content. This is a good place to start, in a lot of cases."

— Teresa Flannery, executive vice president and chief operating officer, CASE, author of *How to Market a University*

The last thing you want to do is duplicate even more effort by creating content that your users already have or can get somewhere else.

Understand Your Audience

We have talked about the importance of knowing your audience in Chapter 3, "Audience First." However, before you start creating anything, you need to make sure you know how the specific content you are going create will help them, what channel(s) you will distribute and promote on, and what action you want them to take. Then you can start planning how you are going to measure the impact.

"Marketing is designed to create exchanges of value between the university and its key stakeholders, and that is most effective when both feel good about the exchange. That is promoted by understanding the needs and values of the people in the target audiences you're trying to reach. And then thinking about what the university's specific offerings are that match those, and where there is a match, to create excellent communication to promote the exchange of value."

— Teresa Flannery, executive vice president and chief operating officer, CASE, author of *How to Market a University*

It is not enough for the content team to understand the audience, it is important that the entire marketing and communications team understands the audience and can help communicate that to stakeholders and leadership. If we are going to be promoting audience-first content and asking for support and collaboration, it is up to us to ensure that everyone involved and everyone supporting the effort also has a solid understanding of the audience's needs.

"We have to be students of marketing and keep up on what's happening, but also what is happening in the broader landscape of higher ed beyond just marketing. I think marketers and communicators can help their institutions navigate this. I think our role in marketing communications is to bring that voice of the consumer to the table."

> — Angela Polec, vice president for strategic marketing and
> communications, Temple University

If you are just starting with content marketing, begin with one audience. Pick the audience that will have the biggest impact. For most institutions, that is typically either potential first-year students or donors.

"You can't be everything to everyone. As a result, it's paramount you are clear on your primary audiences, both who they are and what they need. Focus on your top audiences and strive to provide value in the content you create."

> — Seth Odell, founder and CEO, Kanahoma,
> co-host of *Higher Ed Pulse* podcast

Selling to Leadership

Once you have a solid idea of what you want to do, the content you want to create, and a plan to do it, you need to get buy-in from your leaders. This might just start with convincing your department or school leaders, or it might be institutional leadership you have to convince. It depends on the scope of the strategy you are trying to implement.

"You need leadership support. Leaders need to say, 'Marketing is important. Brand is important. Content strategy is important. We are not going to do this totally decentralized anymore, because it just fractures our message.'"

> — Bill Faust, president, Ologie

If you are taking a proposal for content marketing to leadership, it is essential that you have a solid plan laid out, examples of other peer institutions and even non–higher education brands who are already doing content marketing, and a clear picture of what it will take from a resources and time perspective.

"What helped my department the most was that we had a lot of support from top management. Having their support is essential for other people to believe in what we're doing. But more than anything, it can be a blank card that gives creative freedom. Now more than ever, that's essential to higher education."

> — Emanuel Díaz, head of content marketing, IE University

Do not try to launch a content marketing strategy without leadership support. If you do not have that, you will never be able to commit to the time requirement needed for content marketing to be successful.

Most content marketing plans need at least twelve to eighteen months to start showing impact. That is because it takes time to build a relationship, and that is what content marketing is all about.

"Content and social media are often seen as an afterthought, especially at the C-suite or even the VP level. There's no investment, or there is an assumption that it's not as much of an asset as a billboard. But content can be so much more powerful."

> — Josie Ahlquist, Dr. Josie Ahlquist, Inc.,
> digital engagement and leadership consultant

As you are creating your proposal or presentation for leadership, remember that this is a great opportunity to start practicing content marketing, because that is what you are creating for leadership. You need to show them how content marketing will help solve their problems. How will it be useful and valuable for them?

Have a solid framework and use case in mind. Make sure you are clear up front about the goal of the strategy and the time commitment. Impress upon them how it will connect with the larger marketing and institutional strategies to make it easier for the other programs to continue working.

"One of the challenges is leadership buy-in for this kind of content. It looks and feels very different. People are used to seeing ads that say, 'Apply now,' or 'This is why I came here; you should come here too.' People are used to that kind of content. When there's content without a hard ask, I think it kind of takes people aback a little bit.

So I think it's important to educate leadership on how this looks and feels different, why that is, and how this is part of that overall strategy."

— Carrie Phillips, chief communications and marketing officer,
University of Arkansas at Little Rock

Once you convince your leadership, you may need to convince other teams and departments. Be ready to do road shows and present your strategy to other teams. It is so much easier to be successful with a new content marketing strategy if everyone else knows what you are doing and why. That will additionally create more opportunities for collaboration because they will understand what you are trying to accomplish.

"It's hard because you are going to get pulled in 100 different directions. You are going to be trying to do something, and then there's going to be four straight weeks of annual reports and alumni newsletters. My advice would be to dedicate a team and go hard on internally selling the value of the content and be honest that it's not going to show up right away."

— Nate Jorgensen, senior director of marketing, Miami University

Having leadership support will also help when it comes to saying "no" to other types of content that you have traditionally been creating. If you have to tell some dean why you can not do a story about someone in his department retiring, it is nice to know that your leadership will support you in that decision.

As I said before, it is always good to have alternative methods of support for those other teams, similar to what Purdue has done with the library of assets, resources, and training they have created for the groups they used to do project work for.

"One of the things I tell people, especially when you're talking about marketing and communications strategies and how they need to evolve, is that you need the buy-in of both the executive team and the president to be able to make the decisions and put a stake in the ground that says, 'I don't care what you want, faculty, this is the way that we're going to do the content.' Too many schools don't have that, and they end up wasting too much time. And it wastes marketing dollars, and it wastes efforts."

— Bart Caylor, president and founder, Caylor Solutions,
president, The Higher Ed Marketer, author of *Chasing Mission Fit*

One of the final ways to help convince leadership to support your content marketing strategy is to remind them of all the challenges your institution is facing and show them how content marketing can help overcome these challenges.

"If you don't have a good marketing team to help you tell your story, and if you can't convince your leadership of the importance of telling your story through your content, you are going to find yourself struggling to keep the doors open."

— Dave Tyler, director of university social media,
Rochester Institute of Technology

Start Small

Whenever someone asks me, "How do I start doing content marketing?" I always tell them to start small. Pick one audience, one goal, and one channel.

"Start small. I think it can be intimidating to say, 'Okay, we want to do content marketing, and we want to put together a content marketing strategy and a plan, and then we're going to pitch it.' That can easily become very overwhelming. You start with a few content ideas. We did this when I was at La Salle University and we were just getting into the space. We had a brainstorming session with our admissions team, our marketing team, and our content team and said, 'All right, what do we think prospective students are searching for about college? Not necessarily related to La Salle.' And we just came up with a list of ideas. In the early days, it was not the highest priority of our work. We would find ways to carve out time to put toward those content pieces, and we started with some listicle [an article presented as a list] pieces. Start with one or two pieces and see what that can do. It's one of those things where you are going to learn more by doing than you will by planning."

> — Angela Polec, vice president for strategic marketing and
> communications, Temple University

The key to selecting an audience to target with your first content marketing strategy is to think about where you are most likely to succeed. If this is your proof of concept, you want as big a win as possible.

"Start with your impact. Most institutions don't have enough resources to do what they need to. Make some decisions about prioritizing what kind of content marketing you want to start with. I would start with impact, and what I mean by that is your largest group; most likely, it will be your prospective students."

> — Myla Edmond, senior vice president, RW Jones Agency

The most important thing is to focus on one audience and go niche with that audience. How can you create the best content out there for your audience on a specific topic? Maybe it is prospective students interested in the environment. Maybe it is international students who are looking to find someplace to learn about lasers.

"There has to be a decision and a choice made about which audience you want to speak to with a certain program. Once you have had success there, you can replicate it elsewhere. But the challenge they [institutions] have is they try and do everything at once and it always fails. Because they don't understand which audience they're talking to. They don't give a program enough time to get going."

> — Kyle Campbell, founder and managing director, Education Marketer

Once we understand the power of content marketing and leadership knows the strategy behind what we are doing, we can begin looking for stories to tell and content to create. Do not get in the trap of thinking about channels yet. Instead, start thinking about how you can find someone that is, or was, part of your target audience who has a story of transformation, growth, or change that they can share.

"Content marketing can address whether that student is going to be the hero of their story. Will they become who they aspire to be? Will they be around the type of people that will help them grow into that human? Content marketing supports building brand awareness and standing out in very crowded markets. It supports the engagement of individual students, whether it's recruitment or retention. And it's the community building that happens, because we can't forget about our alumni and donors. When we talk about community building, we also can't forget about our faculty and the really important role that they play. A lot of people are making their decisions based off who they are going to learn from."

— Mallory Willsea, VP marketing, Element451,
chief strategist, Enrollify, co-host of *Higher Ed Pulse* podcast

Think about the journey you want to take your audience on and what stories and content can lead them through it. What are their pain points and concerns on that journey? What questions do they have? Where are the gaps?

"The abundance of advice online about developing a content marketing strategy can be overwhelming, especially for institutions with limited resources. Start simple: assemble your team. Decide what you can realistically handle internally, and how any external partners can help. From there, just take it step by step."

— Melissa Fiorenza, vice president of content strategy,
CCA | Creative Communications Associates

Monitor the content and look to see where they are exiting. How can you change the content you have or create additional content that will help link them through to the next piece? At what point do they reach out to connect or to ask for more?

"Start narrow, learn, iterate, and grow wider. Think about your area of need. Where will this tactic provide the most support or value, and where can you create the best product?"

— Georgy Cohen, director of digital strategy, OHO Interactive

Be Consistent

One thing you will notice about successful content marketing programs is they tend to publish consistently. If you have a podcast, release it at the same time or on the same day every week. You want to build anticipation. You want your user to be waiting for your next piece of content. Once you have that schedule, do not miss it. The first time your user goes to get your next piece of content and it is not there, they will start losing trust in you. And, eventually, they will start looking somewhere else to get what you had been giving them.

"Higher ed has not been great at understanding that their competition in content is not just the university next door. It's every other piece of content in the world. And I would not get daunted with that because the opportunity to reach audiences has also grown. There is space there, and you can leverage it. You need a good team. Start with storytelling, build on it with a good strategy, know your channels, and it can be done."

— Tony Sheridan, senior digital campaigns manager,
KAUST (King Abdullah University of Science and Technology)

Create Vision

Not only is it important to create relationships with your audience, but it is also important to create relationships within your institution. You want to share your vision with other stakeholders and influencers because the more internal support you have, the more opportunities for cross-promotion and resource sharing you will have.

"I am a big believer that people support what they helped create. If there has been a strategic plan developed, and that's followed by a brand strategy that includes value proposition and message, the next step is an institutional content strategy. You create that by going back to the same people who did the strategic plan and worked on the brand strategy and say, 'This is step three, and we want to make sure your school incorporates this overall strategy.' It takes more time, it's more painful, but in the end, it's more sticky, because people were part of it."

— Bill Faust, president, Ologie

Having these relationships will also be necessary when your content marketing starts to pay off and other teams across the institution start asking how they can start their own program or leverage your program to help promote their needs.

"There has to come a point where we stop and think about what offerings and experiences authentically reflect an institution. That is where we are starting to see some institutions take more control of how they're talking about themselves. They are trying to differentiate after years of trying to replicate and be the same as those that they aspire to be.

Now, these marketers and campus leaders are separating and differentiating so they are not seen as the same as everyone else. I see more institutions having tough conversations about who they are and deepening the truthfulness behind how they talk about themselves. Institutions are doing this hard work because the public is demanding it, and they need to find a better way to describe themselves to attract and retain students, faculty, and staff, and generate revenue."

— Teresa Valerio Parrot, EdD, APR, principal, TVP Communications, co-host of *Trusted Voices* podcast

Many institutions are afraid to go too niche. They have so many programs and degree options they want to promote. Yet if you promote everything, you are promoting nothing. You are not doing anything different than so many other institutions.

Find what makes you different and lean into that. The students, faculty, and staff that will be the most successful at your institution are the ones who are the right fit for these specific programs.

"Having a framework is critical. If you are working with an institution to help them with their content strategy, you have to start with a framework. I lean into the StoryBrand principles. The clearest communicator is going to win. Your customer, your target audience, your students are the heroes of that story, the institution is the guide, and they are going to pick you in order to thrive. We need clarity in our differentiation, and just being relentless about showing the individual that they are indeed that hero."

> — Mallory Willsea, VP marketing, Element451,
> chief strategist, Enrollify, co-host of Higher Ed Pulse podcast

Different messaging frameworks can be used for different audiences, or you can use several frameworks with one audience. Some audiences may be a better fit for the Jobs-to-Be-Done (JTBD) framework. Some may resonate more with Donald Miller's StoryBrand framework that leverages the Hero's Journey story structure of Joseph Campbell.

Whether it is the E-E-A-T framework focusing on SEO, the Skyscraper Technique of optimizing and expanding existing content, or the Empathy Map to put yourself in your customer's shoes, there is a framework that can provide the best way to connect with your audience.

All these frameworks can easily be found online. Look into them to determine which one(s) might work best for your audience.

"I have a framework that forces marketers to question how balanced their marketing campaigns are. How much time are you spending letting people know what the heck you're up to? That awareness-raising part should be 25% of what you are doing. Just making sure people are aware of what is happening and what is coming up. The next 25% should be content that supports relationship building. Are you spending enough time really connecting with people? Are we connecting the dots between the institution and their everyday lives? Are we putting that work in? The framework supports another 25% of asking, and 25% follow-up. That's a really nice, balanced approach. But what I usually see is 80% asking, 10% awareness, 5% cultivation, and 5% stewardship. That's how most communication audits play out."

> — Ashley Budd, senior marketing director, Cornell University,
> co-author of *Mailed It: A Guide to Crafting Emails That Build
> Relationships and Get Results*

In the second edition of *Epic Content Marketing*, we talk about the social media 4-1-1 rule. For every six pieces of content you create on a social channel, four pieces of content should be content from your audience that you are sharing or featuring—basically, making your audience the star of your channel—one piece can be your original educational or entertaining content, and one piece can be your sales content promoting a course, offering, or event.

"We have every kind of industry represented on a college campus. We have STEM, we have HR, we have business, and we have healthcare. How can we help our staff build their personal brands around certain themes or topics that our college becomes more associated with in people's minds?"

— Allison Turcio, assistant vice president for enrollment and marketing, Siena College, host of Enrollify's *The Application* podcast

Time Investment

Content marketing is a time investment on several fronts. There is the initial time investment to set it up, assemble the team, research your audience, create your strategy, and plan your content.

Then there is the ongoing time investment in researching and creating new content, repurposing and redistributing existing content, and optimizing high-performing or potentially high-performing content.

Then there is the long-term time investment. When you start a content marketing initiative, we tell people to prepare for a twelve- to eighteen-month commitment. If you are not willing to create valuable content consistently for that amount of time, content marketing may not be for you. There are a lot of short-term, temporary marketing solutions out there that might work just fine—short-term, temporarily.

Choose Your Messengers

A high school junior or senior does not want to hear from some 50-year-old marketer about why they should come to our school. They want to hear from someone their own age, someone who was recently in the same situation they are in now. Someone who "gets" them and knows the issues and decision factors going through their head.

"Students want to hear from other students. They want to bypass the sales pitch for why to come here and get the real insights, the benefits."

> — Karen Freberg, professor of strategic communication,
> University of Louisville, director, The Bird's Nest Student Agency

Not only do our audiences want to hear from other members of that same audience; many of the students, faculty, and staff that we have on our campus want to be content creators or social media influencers. They want to build their personal brand.

Our marketing and communications teams have talented experts in social media, in content creation, in building brands. The opportunity to educate our students, faculty, and staff so they can become vocal supporters of our institution, and themselves, is low-hanging fruit.

"We know that a lot of young people want to become social media influencers or content creators. We see that this is what students want. We see that this is what the business world, or just the world in general, is looking for. There are only a few schools that have social media degrees. We already have everything in place: we have the business, we have accounting, we have English, we have psychology, and all the classes that you would need. It's just packaging. We are going to start seeing more of that."

> — Rob Clark, director of strategic engagement, Greenville University

Several marketing leaders that I spoke with have student-led and -run social teams and even marketing agencies on their campuses. These students get real-world experience with expert guidance, as well as opportunities and knowledge that cannot be taught in the classroom.

"The Bird's Nest is our student-run agency. It's about empowering students to get marketable skills so they are successful after graduation, but we are also able to connect them with community members. Students are creative, they are innovative, they want to show value, and they want to take initiative, especially this generation. They have come forward with brilliant ideas on how to reach students, how to recruit, and how to build the brand. They're going to Instagram, they're going to TikTok, they're doing reels, they're focusing on content. They do research to figure out what works and what doesn't. We started with 14 members when we launched in the fall of 2022. We're now over 32 students. Our clients have ranged from the Kentucky Derby to GE Appliances to Korbel. It's kind of an organic recruiting tool, but it is also empowering student voices."

> — Karen Freberg, professor of strategic communication,
> University of Louisville, director, The Bird's Nest Student Agency

When you suggest an idea like this, many higher education institutions immediately balk at the idea of giving students the reins to their social channels. Some schools work with their students to set up guidelines, some provide training, some review every post before it is posted, and some just trust the students who typically want to do the right thing and are smart enough to follow the lead of the existing posts.

"I don't think the answer is oversight; it's training. A mistake is to underestimate the inherent knowledge and sophistication of young creators. I have met so many extremely impressive young people who are successful creators. They have a business mind. They're not naive. They know what it means to build trust. They know what it means to build an audience. They have a lot of sophistication, more sophistication in digital media than probably anybody in the marketing department at a university. It's really about control and trust. It's got to be training and guidelines and nurturing young creators."

> — Mark Schaefer, executive director, Schaefer Marketing Solutions,
> speaker, author, host of The Marketing Companion podcast

Student creators will make mistakes. There will be things that go out that are not the types of things a seasoned professional might post, and that's okay. We need to provide student creators opportunities to grow and develop their skills. We know that every piece of content that we share will not be a win, but that does not mean we stop putting it out.

Higher education is all about teaching and learning. Real-world experience is a great way for students to learn and grow, and those are the skills that employers are looking for from our graduates.

"If a school wanted to have some influencers involved in creating the curriculum and then layer on top of everything else that you need, I think it would be a no-brainer. Then create an on-campus agency where the students that are in the program actually create the content. They can make money while at college working on their degree doing the thing that they need to learn how to do, and it produces content for the school at scale. There's a huge opportunity there. I think a few schools are going to do that very soon, and they are going to win big."

— Rob Clark, director of strategic engagement, Greenville University

We must remember that our students, faculty, and staff can be some of our most vocal supporters and advocates. They want us to succeed as much as we want them to.

Along with creating content yourself, you should be creating creators! With a little training and oversight, you can create a community of vocal, talented, and authentic influencers who understand and connect with your audiences.

"You have creators on your campus, just go find them. They are going to do it better, more authentically, and faster than any of your staff members. Our students are right at our fingertips. It's just a matter of finding them. The same goes with the faculty members, especially in a graduate environment. If you are not a top-five MBA school, people are probably selecting your institution based on who they are going to be learning from as part of their key criteria. The more you can get your faculty on podcasts, writing, or publishing, the better. The alumni piece goes back to where we started with the institution, allowing the students to aspire to who they want to be. The alumni stories are your best content for showcasing to a prospective or current student, this is who you can aspire to be, because literally, they did it. There is no world where an institution can't be leveraging content creators and think that they are going to continue to do and perform well, from an enrollment standpoint."

> — Mallory Willsea, VP marketing, Element451,
> chief strategist, Enrollify, co-host of *Higher Ed Pulse* podcast

The conversations and engagement that your ambassadors have with students can provide insight into content gaps and connection opportunities that you might never uncover using traditional data mining, surveys, or even interviews.

"In my previous role, when we wanted to promote a postgraduate course, I did not have the dean of sociology talk about it. I had the student that just graduated and landed a great job talk about it. It's so simple, please do it."

> — Tony Sheridan, senior digital campaigns manager,
> KAUST (King Abdullah University of Science and Technology)

Not only are you creating more ways to connect with your target audiences; you are also creating opportunities for your students, faculty, and staff to build their personal brand and make network connections, while promoting the opportunities and benefits of your school.

Potential employers for your students are interested in hiring people with experience. If you have a marketing program and you are not leveraging your student creators and providing them with real-world opportunities, you are both missing out.

"You need to identify a handful of students, talented student creators, who you can work with over the course of their program and beyond. At the moment, it's simply viewed as a tactical device. It's a way to get content out about a certain topic in an accessible way, and we believe that the student voice delivering it is the thing that makes it compelling. I don't think it is. I think it's about building trust in the person delivering it. I think we need a few very strong digital ambassadors that you grow and work with over an extended time to cement their reputation. They essentially become the faces of the brand, and we all know that we're moving away from the corporate 'we' to the individual."

— Kyle Campbell, founder and managing director, Education Marketer

If you can get incoming first-year students who are interested in becoming creators to join an ambassador program, you might have four years of on-the-job training opportunities for them. You could provide them the ability to continuously build and grow their brand and network so that they are ready to step right into a marketing role when they graduate.

"When you are looking at the prospective student, they don't necessarily care about the long-form stories we are telling for reputation building. Social ambassador programs are a good way to go, and it's generally inexpensive for an institution to start one of those up. You are basically paying internship wages for students who really can tell the stories in a way that is going to resonate better with their fellow students. We have seen success in using influencers to get at student populations, as well. I mean, they're there for hire, and they can do a really good job of engaging students as well."

— Jamie Ceman, senior executive vice president, RW Jones Agency

Many of these students will understand the platforms better than we do since they have grown up with them, especially when it comes to social channels. Our students are digital natives and likely spend more time on these channels than we do.

"Some of the best content I have seen from universities comes from when they turn it over to their students. The problem I see is that it's usually just a campaign. It has to be continuous. Something that a lot of people are not talking about is speed. If you want to be relevant on today's social platforms, you basically have an hour a day to be relevant, at most. And the bureaucratic nature of universities, it's just not built for that. The universities that figure out how to be truly relevant on those platforms by taking advantage of the trends and the memes will do that by turning it over to the young people and giving them enough guidelines for them to be free and expressive and creative."

— Mark Schaefer, executive director, Schaefer Marketing Solutions, speaker, author, host of *The Marketing Companion* podcast

Not only can these students create more compelling content for your audiences, they can create more relevant content. These ambassadors are much more aware of the emotional issues first-year students are facing. They know the questions they want to get answered, the things that keep them up at night, and the fear and anxiety they are experiencing.

"This is the biggest decision these young people have made. It's the scariest decision these people are making, and as a teenager, they are already in an emotionally vulnerable place. And it is almost completely unaddressed by universities. The university that learns how to do that will have such an advantage because that's what the students need most at that time in their lives."

— Mark Schaefer, executive director, Schaefer Marketing Solutions, speaker, author, host of *The Marketing Companion* podcast

Another huge benefit of creating creators is that not only will they create content for your channels, they will also create content for their own channels. They will build their personal brands while promoting and advocating for your brand. That sort of content holds more power than any content you put out about yourself.

"Make sure that, wherever possible, your content marketing strategy is not entirely reliant upon the content that you own and create. The reality is that content about your institution that does not exist on your own social channels or your own .edu is going to be far more trusted, rightly or wrongly, than the content that you own. So, content from current students, content from staff, content from alums, content in all the different places that content can live that is about you, but not made by you, has a disproportionate trust level. That's a game I think higher ed needs to play much better than they are today."

— Jay Baer, business growth and customer experience researcher, author, advisor, speaker

Break Down Silos

Content marketing provides the ideal framework to collaborate and coordinate content across an institution. So many of the barriers we have spent years constructing can be removed by starting conversations with other teams about how content can help them and make their jobs easier.

Even better if they do not have to create the content and can just leverage something that someone else is creating and use it to help them reach their goals. They are more connected with their audiences than you are, but you can help them navigate the storytelling and content marketing aspect to make it easy and painless for them.

"I reached out to my colleagues in enrollment management and student affairs to say, 'We want to create more content marketing. I need a group of folks from your two offices to tell us what kinds of things you think students need more guidance on. I need to bring all of us together so we can have those conversations.' Then the other piece is, you get an opportunity to say who can help reinforce whatever messaging we come up with, because it can't just come from your marketing office; it has to be reinforced with the people that the students are going to go to for these answers. If I provide a resource for the students, I am also providing a resource for my colleagues. I often say that marketers are the connectors on campus because so much of our work, even in development, has to depend on us talking to our colleagues. But even reinforcing those messages depends on us talking to our colleagues as well."

— Myla Edmond, senior vice president, RW Jones Agency

Leverage Technology

Technology is disrupting higher education marketing in ways, and at a pace, that we have never seen before. The opportunity to leverage CRM systems and incorporate AI into our marketing gives us incredible access to insights, personalization, and targeting we have never had before.

When we start thinking about how things are going to change due to AR/VR and blockchain technologies, it is difficult to imagine what higher education might look like in five or ten years.

"Marketers are early adopters of technology. We are always looking for ways to improve efficiencies in a way that maybe others on campuses aren't. We are always looking for ways to stand out, and we know that it can't just be on the backs of our teams, because our teams are just not large enough to do the things that we need to. We are always looking for ways that technology can help us do our jobs, and do our jobs better."

— Myla Edmond, senior vice president, RW Jones Agency

We are always facing resource, budget, and staffing issues in higher education. Technologies like AI are going to allow us to do more with less. We might not lose jobs to AI, but we will certainly allow existing staff to be able to accomplish more with the tools and time that they have.

"There are staff retention challenges and hiring challenges in the industry at the moment. We know we are not retaining or attracting the best people. AI is going to create a huge productivity boost and become that persistent assistant to help you get your work done faster."

— Mallory Willsea, VP marketing, Element451,
chief strategist, Enrollify, co-host of *Higher Ed Pulse* podcast

There are always projects we do not have time to get to, or ways we know we can perform better if we could only find the time to adjust our workflows. We know we should be documenting our processes so someone else could perform some of our critical tasks if we were out sick, but we do not have time. Many of those processes could be automated by AI tools.

"AI is going to allow institutions to level up their game and be able to achieve some of the things that we have been talking about, like having a very personalized engagement experience. AI is the transformative technology that is going to let so many schools leapfrog where they are currently to what any individual expects, whether they are 16 or 66. You are going to be more productive, you are going to have better insights. Someone who has no experience at all analyzing data will be able to converse with the system, like a human talking to another human, and just asking questions. [This] will allow people to do more things faster, [including] things that they have never been trained on."

> — Mallory Willsea, VP marketing, Element451,
>   chief strategist, Enrollify, co-host of *Higher Ed Pulse* podcast

These tools will allow us to identify deeper insights from our data, identify opportunities for us, and provide a deeper understanding of our audiences' behavior and needs.

"If you are using a chatbot, you can capture hundreds or thousands of conversations, and AI can help you analyze it and pull out the things that students are asking the most. Then you bring that [data] back into your content marketing planning and strategy. That becomes fodder for updates on your website, handouts at a college fair, and the messages that are going to resonate with students at different parts of their journey. The conversations will become a gold mine for directing your content marketing efforts.

Just as important is that your best human engagement strategy can never be 24/7, because we cannot be 24/7. That is our limitation. That is not a limitation of AI. An AI-powered chatbot allows you to be where the student needs you, when they need you, with the right answer to the question that they have. The chatbot is going to become critical because it's going to take humans out of the process where they don't need to be and ensure that the instant response happens for each individual."

> — Mallory Willsea, VP marketing, Element451,
>   chief strategist, Enrollify, co-host of *Higher Ed Pulse* podcast

EPIC THOUGHTS

- Start by thoroughly understanding the institutional strategy, target audiences, and goals the content marketing effort needs to support. Conduct a content audit to identify gaps and opportunities. Pick one priority audience to focus on initially.

- Assemble a team with the right skills, especially storytelling, and create a documented content marketing strategy and mission statement. Get leadership buy-in by showing how content marketing will solve their problems and allow time for the strategy to work.

- Consistently create and deliver the most relevant, valuable content possible for the target audience. Establish an editorial calendar but stay agile to optimize based on performance data. Break down silos by collaborating with other teams on audience insights and distribution.

- Empower and showcase authentic student, faculty, and alumni voices in your content, as they are trusted more than official university messages. Identify and nurture talented student creators/influencers who can build their own brands while supporting yours.

CHAPTER 10

Content Types

When we talk about the content landscape, there are lots of ways we can create and deliver content. You have a lot of options and variations of text, audio, visual, or video content. Of course, there are even more channels that we can put our content on.

Each of the different content types and channels could have an entire book dedicated to it, and many of them do. I am not going to dive into the basics of each one, but I want to point out how some of these can be used effectively in higher education content marketing.

One thing that is important to remember when distributing content is the difference between "owned land" and "rented land." Owned land includes content types where you control the data and distribution (like a newsletter), while rented land includes content types where your content is posted to a property you do not own (like social media). When thinking about distribution, remember that control and data matter.

It's great if you have a million followers on TikTok, but if the platform gets shut down or your account gets suspended, you have no way to recapture that audience. They might come find you on another channel, but you have no recourse to reach out to them.

On the other hand, if you have 20,000 people subscribing to your newsletter and the newsletter tool you have been using gets acquired or shuts down, you can export your list of subscribers, take that to another system, and you are back in business.

When using rented land you also have limited access to your data and distribution. You are at the mercy of the platform when it comes to what metrics they share and what you can use to discover insights, and you have very little control over who sees your content. You are reliant on the whims of the algorithm.

When you are putting your content on rented land, just keep this in mind and always be thinking of ways to drive that audience to an owned property (like a newsletter).

There are also nontraditional channels for content marketing. These are places we do not typically think of as content marketing channels, but the content we put on those channels can be leveraged to support our content marketing efforts.

Owned Land

We will start by talking about the content types and channels that we own and control. Most of the content we create is targeted for digital delivery, but it is important to remember that people have been creating and distributing content before the Internet and that many of those analog methods are still extremely effective.

"It's all about those owned spaces, those owned channels. We can always own channels like email and our websites. Community-based platforms that schools can own and leverage to operate the way they want are something to look forward to."

— Harrison "Soup" Campbell, head of community experience, ZeeMee

News Stories

Many higher education institutions have some sort of news content that is served up regularly. This is a perfect place to create meaningful, long-form content that can connect with audiences and establish you as a leader in your strategic areas.

It is important to remember, with every story you post, that this content is not all about your institution. It is about how your institution and the people who work there are impacting the world, changing lives, and innovating.

There are numerous ways to structure and target these sites, but one of the best things you can do is to think about who you are talking to. Boston University has done this by segmenting its news content into three different sites—BU Today, The Brink, and The Bostonia.

BU Today targets the campus community and features coverage of events, profiles of faculty, staff, students, and alumni, and other items and stories of interest to their community.

The Brink features research stories from BU and primarily targets external audiences who are interested in cutting-edge research.

The Bostonia is the alumni magazine featuring profiles and stories about, or of interest to, BU alumni.

One of the reasons this segmenting is so effective for the university is that individual news stories are shared across the platforms so that the specific audiences will not miss anything they are interested in, but do not have to sort through stories that are not relevant or helpful.

Blogs

Blogs differ from news stories because they tend to be more first-person content, more informal and opinionated, and cover a variety of topics. News stories tend to be third-person and more focused on specific events, achievements, or announcements.

Blogs can be text and image formats on a website, or they can be vlogs (video blogs), which can be hosted in a variety of places.

Blogs provide a great format for members of a specific audience to share and connect with other members of that audience. As we said in the last chapter, choosing your messengers is critical to creating epic content marketing, and blogs provide an excellent way to provide a platform to those messengers.

Miami University's Division of Student Life blog features stories from students and alumni that are targeted at helping other students navigate the ins and outs of the student experience.

Newsletters

One of the best ways to connect with an audience is through newsletters. Newsletter users typically subscribe to receive content from you. However, some schools automatically subscribe new students, faculty, or staff to the institutional newsletter, which makes it even more critical to ensure that your content is relevant and valuable.

"A newsletter can be executed well for specific audiences, but how do we take it from 'this is what is happening' to 'here is something that is beneficial for you'? Storytelling is important, but let's not just tell stories. Let's provide tactical takeaways."

> — Jackie Vetrano, assistant director, prospect management and
> marketing, UNC Kenan-Flagler Business School

Newsletters can be more than just links to important items happening around the campus and aggregates of different news content. They can provide a perspective to those stories and can help curate and segment those stories for different audiences.

"I have been chasing the industry newsletter model for higher ed. I figured out how to be better than political emails, how to be better than other nonprofits, and how to be better than other higher education institutions, but I have not figured out how to be better than this industry news model. And it's because industry newsletters are so helpful. They are invested in their readers' success. They want to help you right now. There is something for us to learn in that. Why do so many people subscribe to other institutional news, like the *Harvard Business Review* or the *MIT Technology Review*? They are not alumni of these institutions. It's because they're serving great content."

> — Ashley Budd, senior marketing director, Cornell University,
> co-author of *Mailed It: A Guide to Crafting Emails That Build
> Relationships and Get Results*

The University of Pennsylvania has several newsletters with various delivery options including a daily or weekly edition of *Penn Today*, as well as a weekly P*enn Today for Parents*, specifically curated to parents of students.

Infographics

Being able to summarize data in a visual and easy-to-understand way makes infographics incredibly useful. A well-designed and informative infographic (with your logo or name on it) can get lots of engagement and visibility within your target audience, so be sure to make it as shareable as possible. Infographics can be a great way to showcase original research.

Webinars

A webinar series can be an effective way to consistently engage with audiences on particular areas of interest. A well-thought-out webinar can provide an enormous amount of content that can be reused across channels and in various formats. It can be delivered as a live event, used as an on-demand event, and broken out into smaller clips for sharing on social.

Virtual Tours

Protecting people from Covid-19 drove many schools to create virtual campus tours, and virtual tours have continued to be important ways to connect with prospective students who may be considering your school. These tours can be more than just ways to see what the campus looks like and where things are. They can be an opportunity to share stories from other students, connect prospects with resources, and begin to build a sense of connection with the institution before students ever set foot on campus.

Digital and Print Magazines

Magazines can be a great way to stay connected with key audiences. Many institutions have print or digital magazines that they send to all their alumni to keep them updated on things happening on campus and within the alumni community.

Rented Land

Social Media

Social media is an excellent place to connect with new and existing audiences. Different platforms work better than others for specific audiences. LinkedIn is excellent for building awareness with prospective faculty and researchers, Facebook can be a great place to connect with parents and alumni, while TikTok and Instagram tend to work well when connecting with current and prospective students.

"In higher ed, we have always chased rented audiences with social platforms. You don't own the community or any of the data behind the community. All Meta is ever going to give you is vanity metrics. We have built communities on these platforms, but it's tough when you don't own it. Use Twitter [X] as an example. Many of us had these great communities we were a part of, and all it took was new ownership coming in and wreaking havoc to show us how quickly it could change. The whole reason social media began was for relationships, connection, and community. Unfortunately, the traditional model for social platforms to monetize and generate revenue is because they have to transition to ad platforms, and now it's no longer an actual social platform."

— Harrison "Soup" Campbell, head of community experience, ZeeMee

Social platforms can provide a lot of engagement opportunities, and social listening can provide numerous insights into your brand perception and create opportunities to address issues before they become problems.

Video

Yes, video can exist on your website. It can be embedded on pages, and it can be linked to from newsletters and email, but videos typically live on platforms like YouTube, Vimeo, or within social platforms like Reels, YouTube Shorts, or TikTok, which is why they are in rented land.

Video content tends to be highly engaging, especially with younger audiences. Video is the ultimate content type for repurposing as one video can be used to create a podcast, blog posts, or multiple vertical short-form videos for social media and can be added to your website.

Podcasts

Like video, podcasts can also exist on your website, but, for the greatest distribution, these are typically hosted on a platform that controls distribution and limits access to data.

Podcasts tend to be slow avenues to grow an audience, but they provide an excellent way to maintain a connection with an existing audience.

Nontraditional Content Marketing

There are various types of content we create that we tend not to associate with content marketing because they lack the consistency we generally value. However, these mediums can also be leveraged to support our content marketing if we are aware of our content marketing strategy and how that may connect to our overall content strategy.

Websites

Our websites tend to be our largest entry point for most audiences. The ability to deliver our brand message, capture target users, and share our stories through our web content is massive.

Yet, many schools are not using their websites as intentionally as they could be. That can cause the website to quickly become an information dumping ground that is difficult to navigate to find useful content.

As you are creating content for your website, think about the larger content strategy and content marketing strategy. Look for ways to integrate valuable content for specific audiences and include calls to action to encourage them to continue their journey through the site or engage with the content in some way, whether as simple as playing an embedded video or as valuable as filling out a request for information.

Emails

We tend to fall back on email communications regularly, especially in times of crisis or to distribute leadership messages. We also send emails for upcoming deadlines or announcements. And, of course, we send emails as part of any marketing automation program we manage.

Most marketing emails that we send as part of a campaign have a hard ask or call to action that the entire message is focused on.

"We are sending emails to people because we want them to do something. We want students to apply, we want alumni to make a gift. We want staff to update their two-factor authentication. But if we think of email as a channel for content marketing, it will also change what we send people. Why aren't we sending engaging content that is relevant to our readers in between, or in addition to, all these call-to-action emails? Email could be a fantastic channel for content marketing if we treat it as a way to build relationships and create value for our readers, and not just send what we want to send."

> — Dayana Kibilds, strategist, Ologie, speaker, co-author of *Mailed It: A Guide to Crafting Emails That Build Relationships and Get Results*, host of Enrollify's *Talking Tactics* podcast

Syndicating

Having one of our news stories picked up by a large publication is a great way to help increase brand awareness and visibility. It will often lack any direct link back to your owned channels and will typically exclude any call to action you included, but it can be an excellent way to attract attention and connect with new audiences.

As you put out news content, always be thinking about what publications might be interested in sharing your content with their audiences.

Speaking

Public speaking at large events and conferences is an excellent way to not only build a personal brand but to increase awareness and authority of the institutional brand.

"There is a huge opportunity for faculty to become influencers. Everyone has the power of influence. Everyone has the ability to share and coach. The knowledge is just about packaging it right. As an industry, we do not utilize our faculty the way they could be showcased in our content. There are some faculty that don't want to be bothered by content. But others have their own following, they see the benefit, and they want to build up their reputation."

> — Karen Freberg, professor of strategic communication,
> University of Louisville, director, The Bird's Nest Student Agency

There are numerous opportunities for faculty, staff, and students at an institution to present at events and share their knowledge while representing the institution.

Campus Tours

In-person tours can often be the deciding factor on a prospect's decision to choose an institution or not. The choice is often fraught with anxiety and emotion because it can be one of the first major decisions in a person's life and can have a huge impact on their future.

"It is really interesting to me that one of the largest investments that a person will make in their life, the cost of higher education, is far too often sold by a 23-year-old with very little sales training."

> — Bart Caylor, president and founder, Caylor Solutions,
> president, The Higher Ed Marketer, author of *Chasing Mission Fit*

The campus tour is often the first time a person has an opportunity to connect with someone at the school and to get an understanding of the campus culture.

"One thing that really scares me is the preponderance of students, high school juniors and seniors, who are choosing a school based on vibes. Higher ed institutions put way too little emphasis on tours and who does the tour, and what is said. And what the experience [is] of that tour. And how do you make it differentiated and memorable from all the other schools these kids and their parents are visiting? Given how important it is, in terms of vibe check, I would be increasing that budget by 6x. My goal would be to be the greatest tour in America and figure out a way to make that happen. That's what I would do."

> — Jay Baer, business growth and customer experience researcher,
> author, advisor, speaker

EPIC THOUGHTS

- When choosing content types and distribution channels, prioritize "owned land" like websites, newsletters and blogs where you control the data and distribution, versus "rented land" like social media where you have less control and access to audience data.

- Newsletters can be powerful for delivering curated, valuable content to subscribed audiences, not just institutional updates. Look to industry newsletter models for inspiration on focusing content around helping readers succeed.

- Measure the impact of content marketing efforts in both owned and rented channels, but do not build your strategy around vanity metrics from social platforms. Use the deeper insights from owned channels to optimize content that builds relationships.

CHAPTER 11

Discoverability

How your content gets discovered is critically important to your overall performance. You can create the best content out there and have the solution to every one of your audience's problems, but it will not matter how good it is if they do not find it.

Historically, search engine optimization (SEO) was the primary way to target organic traffic. SEO is all about creating your content in a way that ensures search engines will find it and feature it when users are looking for that content.

According to Meltwater's 2024 State of Digital research, the primary reason users aged 16 to 64 go on the Internet is to find information, and 80% of those users go to search engines or portals to get that information.

"Being top of mind and having your content come into a student's sphere, or anyone's sphere, organically and authentically, is super important."

— Jenny Li Fowler, director of social media strategy, MIT, author of *Organic Social Media: How to Build Flourishing Online Communities*, host of Enrollify's *Confessions of a Higher Ed Social Media Manager* podcast

Getting ranked by search engines for strategically important terms is an ongoing process that involves researching keywords that are driving traffic to that type of content, understanding what questions users are asking about those topics, looking at your content landscape to see what you could create that would provide answers to those questions, and then creating that content in a way that features those keywords in all the right places.

If you do that better than the websites that are currently ranking for those terms, you can oftentimes take over those top positions.

"An opportunity in content marketing for higher ed is that we have built-in authority. If you have a .edu, you are already head and shoulders above almost any new organization, institution, or any new website that is rolling up—even something with a body of content that's thousands of pages deep, higher ed's authority almost always outranks."

— Tim Jones, director, brand and integrated strategy,
  SimpsonScarborough

If you can get to the number one search position for certain terms, you can capture what is called a featured snippet, which is where Google puts your content above all the search results (paid and organic) and showcases your answer.

These featured snippets are also known as zero-click results. The reason Google features these is because they want to provide the answer right from their site so users do not click and go somewhere else.

While they may not drive traffic to your site, featured snippets do position you as the experts around the particular subject, and there are inherent brand benefits to that sort of prominence. They also often feed alternative search methods like voice search.

SEO, by itself, is not enough anymore. Targeting content for performance on typical search engines no longer ensures that your content is found by the audience you are creating it for, especially if that audience is Gen Z or Gen Alpha.

Our prospective students are using different means of search like voice search, social search, and AI-powered search. We need to start thinking about making our content discoverable and optimized for these new search methods.

A study from Search Engine Land predicted that websites could lose anywhere from 18% to 64% of their organic traffic due to SGE (search generative experience) or AI-powered search.[1]

We need to start thinking about AI search optimization and AEO (answer engine optimization), which focus more on getting your content in the most consumable format and on the right channels so it will be indexed and returned by these technologies.

Look at all the places where users are seeking answers, including social channels, video channels, and community channels like Reddit and Quora. Start thinking about how to get your best content into those channels and how to change your workflow to begin including content for those channels. Then, learn how to start optimizing your content for those channels.

There are two different ways to think about doing content optimization: reactive and proactive.

"So many of these marcom offices are stuck in this reactive model versus being proactive, or more strategic. That's where content marketing comes in. It is a more proactive model where you are saying, 'We have an opportunity or we have a problem, and we have decided that content marketing is the right tactic'. Shifting to the proactive model is hard if you have been in a reactive model. A lot of that is political. A lot of that is decades of legacy expectation. The shift into a proactive model comes from a change in leadership."

— Georgy Cohen, director of digital strategy, OHO Interactive

Reactive

Reactive content optimization begins with determining what content you have already created is performing well in organic traffic or is ranking for high-volume or strategically relevant search terms.

You discover this by looking at your data. Google Analytics and Google Search Console are the first places to start with reactive optimization. If you have a paid SEO tool like Semrush, Moz, Ahrefs, or Majestic, those tools are designed to help you figure out where your best opportunities are.

However, Google Analytics and Google Search Console can provide a lot of insights to get you started. Look at what content is driving consistent organic traffic to your site and see what keywords people are searching to find your site.

Next, you go to those pages and add those keyword phrases to your content in a few more places. Ideally, you want to include them in your headlines, body copy (though not too often or Google will flag you for spamming), links, anchor text, image names (using hyphens to separate the words, i.e., content-marketing.jpg), alt tags (accessibility first, but include keywords if they make sense), and add additional content that answers some of the common questions that are being asked around that topic.

You can use a tool like Yoast, which is a free plug-in for most CMS programs, to help with the optimization, and you can use resources like answerthepublic.com to get ideas about additional questions to include. You can also simply go to Google and look at the People Also Ask questions they feature.

Proactive

Proactive content optimization is when you look at what topics are trending and what conversations are happening and you leverage your expertise to create content around those topics.

Google Trends can be helpful with this, as well as online communities like Reddit, but the best way is to be familiar with the expertise at your institution and look for topical opportunities to create in-demand content that features them.

Social Search

To target social search, you need to create content to distribute on those channels. Use relevant hashtags to make your content more findable and create content that is focused on the audience you are targeting on each platform.

Communities

Online discussion communities like Reddit or niche communities (most often on platforms like Discord, Slack, or Circle) are typically places that frown on active marketing or pitching, so make sure you only engage with these communities from a place of information sharing and answering questions, not promoting your school or programs.

Establishing yourself and your institution as an expert in different topical areas can help build trust with the audience there and can often drive substantial traffic to your website.

AI-Powered Search

Generative AI search and social media search are changing the face of SEO. Industry experts are claiming that SGE (search generative experience) may impact organic traffic as much as 18% to 60% for most businesses. Therefore, if your current strategy is built around users coming to your site from traditional search engines like Google, it is time to start rethinking that tactic.

We do not yet fully understand how generative AI discovers and features particular content, but the way LLMs (large language models) work is by looking at their dataset and attempting to predict what the best next word, image pixel, or video frame will be.

Thus, the key is to have the best content about a particular topic and to have that content in as many places as you can.

More and more of these generative AI search tools are citing the sources of their information because people do not trust the tools themselves. And you shouldn't, at least not yet. These tools still tend to make things up when they don't know, instead of just telling you they don't.

However, these tools create new opportunities for conversational and personalized search in a way that traditional search engines cannot deliver. Starting to think about how we create content in order to best leverage this new technology will be the key to appearing in the results.

"We can go into Claude or ChatGPT and say, 'I want to study at a university where I can be near the mountains, and in a culture that is extremely inclusive. I identify as being LGBTQ+. I'm fascinated by economics, but I'm really fascinated in the economics of sub-Saharan Africa, and I like a temperature climate that somewhere between 25 and 35 degrees Celsius.' We can just chat that and it's going to give you a very reliable list of institutions. If we are not providing and creating the content that shows that these things are relevant to our institutions, especially on the values-based stuff, then we are not going to come up. We can't rely on the clunky old filtering process anymore. It's a lot more sophisticated.

For those of us in the UK and in the US, Canada, Australia, these English-speaking countries, there are some serious threats to us in the market coming from countries that offer incredible programs that people don't necessarily look at, but actually might be in particular cultures that have a really strong values-based system, or a particularly strong cultural identity. And that suddenly will become a lot easier for people to think about going to those locations, because it's opened up to them by looking and thinking about searching for universities in very different ways."

— Tracy Playle, chief content strategist, Pickle Jar Communications, author of *The Connected Campus*

EPIC THOUGHTS

- While SEO remains important, it is no longer enough on its own to ensure that content gets discovered by target audiences, especially younger generations. Institutions must also optimize content for voice search, social search, and AI-powered search.

- Higher education websites have a built-in authority advantage in search rankings due to their .edu domains. Strategically creating the best content on key topics can help secure valuable "featured snippets" that appear above all other search results.

- Institutions should take both a reactive approach, optimizing existing high-performing content, and a proactive approach, creating new content around trending topics that leverage in-house expertise, to improve search discoverability.

- As generative AI search grows, institutions must adapt by creating the best possible content on their key topics and distributing it widely. Showcasing unique offerings, values, and experiences in content will be critical to surface in increasingly personalized AI-powered search results.

EPIC RESOURCES

1. Gilad David Maayan, "How Google SGE will impact your traffic – and 3 SGE recovery case studies," Search Engine Land, September 5, 2023, https://searchengineland.com/how-google-sge-will-impact-your-traffic-and-3-sge-recovery-case-studies-431430

CHAPTER 12

Repurposing and Redistributing

The best advice from content marketing experts has always been: start with one platform where you can be the best and establish yourself there before beginning to expand to other channels. Now, with generative AI tools, you can repurpose, reimagine, and redistribute your content to a variety of channels with less work than ever before.

"There are people who should be worried about AI taking their jobs. Those [people] who aren't dynamic, who cannot or will not change, should be worried. It's a situation of change or be changed. I can see it opening a world of opportunities."

> — Tony Sheridan, senior digital campaigns manager,
> KAUST (King Abdullah University of Science and Technology)

The additional capabilities created by AI tools will provide efficiencies that will change our workflows. Tasks will take longer initially as we figure out how to use the tools most effectively, but later the time-savings will enable us to focus our efforts on other areas, like creativity and strategy. We must be careful, however, to monitor the output from AI to ensure that we are not improving productivity at the cost of connection.

"AI both excites and worries me. I think it has great potential to help us to speed and scale up our marketing and communication efforts, however, I think we can lose the personal touch if we are not careful of actually engaging with another human being. There is already a lack of personalization in higher ed, where often we see people as leads and send out hundreds of thousands of bulk emails, "Hi [first_name]" without properly learning about what each prospective student needs and building a real relationship. AI can help with hyper-personalization, but not to the point where an actual person has taken an interest in each prospective student and knows their name, interests, hopes, and fears of joining their university. AI can help us, but the human touch and engagement are desperately needed."

— Philip Smith, founder and CEO, Education Marketing Agency

Beyond changing the way we market and create content, AI will change the way we learn new skills and do our work. AI agents will become personal assistants that will be able to add value or make suggestions while we work and perform our tasks.

AI will identify areas of efficiency that we do not see, and we will need to be able to collaborate with these tools in order to excel at our work.

"It will go beyond the degree, and not just in terms of affinity or pride or relationship. The only way to AI-proof your job is to stay educated and keep developing the human skills that will pair with what AI brings to the table. We have to think about education in a lifetime and holistic way so that we are prepared for the future of work."

— Allison Turcio, assistant vice president for enrollment and marketing, Siena College, host of Enrollify's *The Application* podcast

Repurposing

It is as important as ever to begin your content marketing with one primary platform. It might be a blog, it might be your news site, or even a YouTube channel. Regardless of which channel you select, create your content for that channel in a way that provides the most opportunity for the reuse of that content.

We must start thinking omnichannel with our content creation. The process should focus on the content itself, the story, and the message, not the delivery method or channel. As you go through the content selection process and start getting into the creation phase, think about all the places you can use the content, what elements you will need for those different places, and how your creation process can provide you with those assets without having to duplicate effort.

We have to start thinking about repurposing as we create, not after.

"In the higher ed world, we overcomplicate and slow things down. The biggest hurdle is that we have to realize that speed is going to be what wins. Speed allows us to make content at scale. We have the opportunity and infrastructure to be putting out 20 pieces of content per day, whereas most [competitors] will put out one or two."

— Rob Clark, director of strategic engagement, Greenville University

We need to start thinking about all the content we create and how we can repurpose it for different uses that might be helpful to other audiences. Are we creating internal training for our staff on things like accessibility or analytics that could have best practices or a checklist pulled out and shared on social?

"One of the most underutilized capabilities in higher ed marketing is repackaging course content. It's rare to see course content repurposed so a student can try it. We live in an age where you can access education, a lot of it for free, via YouTube, and it's best in class. We are supposed to have the premier education offer, and all our rankings and all our testimonials say so, but we don't let anyone see it until they arrive on campus. This seems bizarre to me. We are starting to see taster sessions that repurpose elements of courses as recruitment on-ramps. I think this will become the new course video. I also think we will start to see a lot more shorter courses. There is an emphasis right now on lifelong learning, and that does not necessarily take the shape of a four-year campus-based program. It's much more piecemeal."

— Kyle Campbell, founder and managing director, Education Marketer

Redistributing

It is always wonderful to see a particular piece of content performing well, or to see users finding real value from a piece of content you have shared. Sometimes we will go back to that content and optimize it to perform better on search, but how often do we think about how we can take that valuable content and redistribute it on other channels, to other audiences, or in a different format?

Whenever you are redistributing content, you always have to remember the audience you are targeting on the new channel and the best practices for that channel to ensure you are delivering it in the most relevant, compelling, and high-performing way.

"How can content that researchers are creating be repurposed into something more universal, more accessible to other audiences? How can we translate what they are doing into podcasts or blogs, or just a robust presence on LinkedIn? The right channel is not just where the audience might be, but what the faculty members are comfortable with and then getting them to think about the content in different ways. We publish this journal article, but along the way, what can we be saying about the research you did that got to that article? Then, how can we repurpose your findings into different kinds of stories that you can tell to a wider audience? The thing about higher ed is that there is already that content. Throw a rock, you are going to hit an expert on a college campus. So how do we leverage these experts into content that is more universal and accessible to wider audiences, that generates reputational value for the college, and for the person to build their personal brand? This is a people-centered approach to building a reputation."

— Allison Turcio, assistant vice president for enrollment and marketing, Siena College, host of Enrollify's *The Application* podcast

How often do we see a piece of high-performing content and decide that we need to turn it into an infographic or a video? Why do we believe that particular format is the only way content will be successful? Think of each piece of content you distribute as a test to see if that story resonates or if that information is helpful. If it is, use it again.

This is where we need to start thinking about the value of our content. Think of your content like a product, the way media companies do. If you look at a manufacturer who has a product that is successful in one market, they do not think, "Good, now let's go make something completely new." No, they think, "Where else can we sell this? Who else needs this? How can we make it better?" That is what we need to do with our content. We need to respond to the input we are getting from our users.

"It's about creating a culture of responsiveness more than raw speed. Audit the elapsed time at each of the steps in different funnels and then ask how we shave that down. People's comfort with waiting and elapsed time is really low now, and I think the pace in higher ed is increasingly at odds with how the rest of the world thinks about time and responsiveness. I would ask people in higher ed to justify any delay in getting back to people and ask why this is a better approach."

— Jay Baer, business growth and customer experience researcher, author, advisor, speaker

As you identify successful content to redistribute, think about other channels you might be able to start leaning into with topical content. If you identify several pieces of successful content on a particular topic that seem to have an audience, maybe there is enough related information that could feed a podcast series that you could link to from the different high-performing content pieces.

"Schools should start playing with content marketing. Pick a couple of channels, dive into those, and see where it can take you. I think podcasts are low-hanging fruit for content marketing. As you think about starting, think about ways you can repurpose that content."

— Jaime Hunt, chief marketing officer, Old Dominion University, host of *Confessions of a Higher Ed CMO* podcast

Personalizing and Targeting

Integrating AI into our martech stack is going to provide us with methods to hyper-personalize our content in ways we cannot imagine.

Every piece of data that we receive from a potential student or faculty will help us deliver the most relevant content and messaging to them.

"We are going to see the death of campaigns and anything campaign-ish. The student, the parent, the staff member, or whoever the key audience is, will only be getting email, direct mail, whatever that is created specifically based on what we know about them, delivered to them as an audience of one. The data shows that hyper-personalization tends to yield better outcomes, and it's totally doable now.AI is just going to make it smarter and easier. I would ask people to defend sending more than one thing at a time. If you send more than one thing, you are essentially saying: we do not have the data to be hyper-personalized, we do not have the budget, or we do not have the manpower. All those objections are fading away very quickly."

— Jay Baer, business growth and customer experience researcher,
author, advisor, speaker

EPIC THOUGHTS

- Generative AI tools offer new opportunities to efficiently repurpose, reimagine, and redistribute content across multiple channels. While AI can improve productivity, institutions must monitor output quality and avoid losing human touch and personal engagement.

- Content creation processes should be omnichannel from the start, focusing on the core story and message, not just the initial delivery channel. Planning for repurposing during creation, rather than after, is key to avoiding duplicate effort.

- Successful content should be continually redistributed to new channels and audiences in different formats. Looking at content as a product to be reused and improved based on performance data, like media companies do, is a shift higher education needs to make.

- Repurposing academic content like research and courses into more accessible, public-facing formats like podcasts, blogs, and taster sessions can generate reputational value for faculty and the institution while supporting enrollment and lifelong learning.

- AI will enable hyper-personalization of content for each individual based on their data and behaviors. Mass campaigns will fade away in favor of tailored "audience of one" communications delivered through the right mix of channels for each person.

CHAPTER 13

Tracking and Optimizing

"What gets measured gets managed—even when it is pointless to measure and manage it, and even if it harms the purpose of the organization to do so."

— V. F. Ridgway [1]

We have access to so much data in higher education that it can be paralyzing to figure out what we should be collecting, analyzing, and acting on. This is where processes can help. We need to have a solid understanding of what we are trying to do and then know how we are going to measure success.

"We can't just put stuff out into the universe and think it's great. We have to learn and iterate as we go. We have to think about measurement, about content that is purpose-driven and brand-aligned, and not just chuck ideas out into the stratosphere. Understand that you are going to try some stuff and it won't work. Then you will try other stuff. That is the importance of the measurement piece. The most important thing, besides the focus and goal piece, is making sure that the organization, culturally and process-wise, understands the need to monitor and optimize. We are not going to get it perfect from the get-go. We're not done, we're just starting."

— Georgy Cohen, director of digital strategy, OHO Interactive

Anytime I start a new website optimization project, I follow a process. It always begins with clearly defining and understanding the strategy. What are you trying to accomplish? What are the goals? What will indicate success? The key to clearly understanding what you are trying to do is to ask "Why?" a lot.

This generally takes the form of a discussion with senior leaders. Typically, you go as senior as you can. If you are optimizing a department website, you want to be talking to the head of the department. If it is a school, you should be talking with the dean of the school. If it is an institutional site, you should be talking with VPs/AVPs and, if possible, the president.

Oftentimes, institutions will have a strategic plan documented on the website along with mission statements and value propositions. These are all critical documents to have and to understand before having a conversation with leaders, but they do not replace the conversation. The function of the website within the strategic landscape often has a very different implementation or function than other areas.

Strategic Audit

You want to walk away from the strategic audit with a solid understanding of what the website should be doing and how we will know if it has been successful. Without this fundamental knowledge, you cannot start thinking about OKRs (objectives and key results) and KPIs (key performance indicators)or know how to set up tracking or what you need to be measuring.

Figure 13-1. The Website Optimization Process

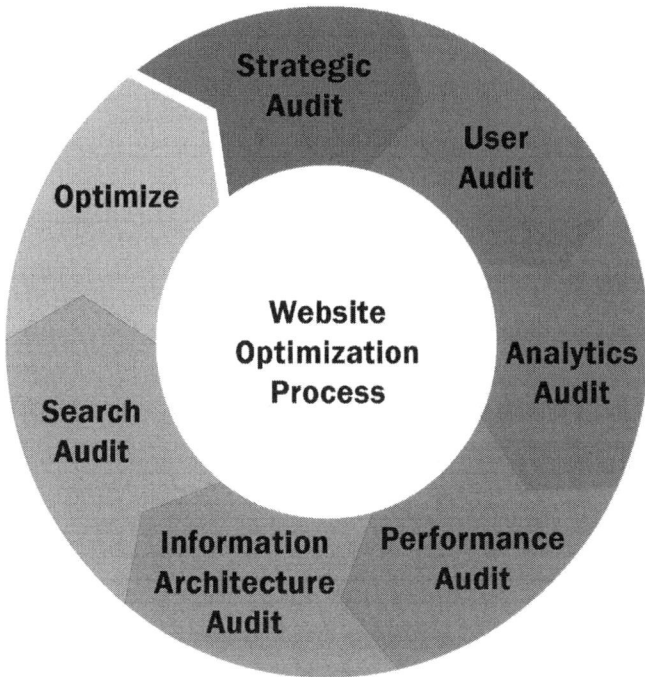

User Audit

The second phase is the user audit. This is where you figure out what audiences you need to be targeting to accomplish each of the strategic goals. Some goals may have multiple audiences, so you need to figure out how you can differentiate between the audiences when it comes to how each one can help you reach your goals.

The user audit is the time to start talking about personas. What data do you already have that can help you understand the specifics around who you are talking to? You may not need to invest the resources into creating specific marketing, buyer, and audience personas at this point, but you do need to know who you are talking to and what you are going to want them to do for you to reach your goals.

Analytics Audit

Next is the analytics audit. Does the website have the correct measurement accounts set up, and are they configured properly? Does the site have Google Analytics 4, Google Tag Manager, and Google Search Console, or comparable substitutes? These are the minimums. Without these, you cannot accurately measure or track performance. Once you determine that the right tools are in place, and are set up correctly, you can start collecting data.

This is when you will need KPIs and OKRs identified if you did not do it during the strategic audit. The data you are going to collect will measure those KPIs so you can track progress. You may have to set up custom events or conversions to accurately track the behaviors and outcomes.

Depending on how granular you are going to get, you may need custom tags, triggers, and data layer variables. Remember, these elements only start tracking after you set them up, so now is the time to get everything configured properly.

This is the time to start getting your baseline for content performance and, when you look at the existing data, to identify patterns and anomalies. For a new site, I typically look back over one year (and sometimes three years, depending on the type of content) to identify high-performing content.

This is often a good time to set up a dashboard with your KPIs and other general performance metrics. Along with tracking KPIs, I often track things like high-performing content by views and users (direct and organic), traffic sources and mediums, campaign performance, search performance, and audience data.

"It's important to have a dashboard that shows the results of the content strategy and how certain stories, certain content, don't just benefit one audience; they benefit a broad audience and multiple units."

— Bill Faust, president, Ologie

Performance Audit

The next audit is a performance audit. You need to know how the site is functioning technically for both search engines and the users. Is it loading fast? Do elements move around when the site loads on mobile? Is the site secure? Are there broken links or deprecated code on the site?

There are a lot of tools that can help with this process, but Google Search Console has an entire section on Experience that includes things like Core Web Vitals. These can be very technical issues, but they can have a huge impact on search performance as well as user experience. Some of these items can be quick fixes that have significant impact, while some can be symptoms of the CMS or template that can be difficult to address. You have to pick and choose what will create the biggest return.

The main thing is that you must look at the data. You will never know what opportunities you are missing or what issues you are causing for your users or search engines if you do not look at the data.

"A real deficit in higher ed is the internal capacity for monitoring and reporting—whether it's SEO or analytics, there is a gap. Some schools have a dedicated person, but most have analytics just running in the background like a refrigerator. Success is going to come from having a proactive focus and from being purpose-driven."

— Georgy Cohen, director of digital strategy, OHO Interactive

Information Architecture Audit

Next we get to the information architecture audit. How is your content structured? How is it organized? How many levels deep is your site? Are your strategically valuable pages easy to find? Are users using your navigation?

Search engines and users both prefer flatter sites. A flatter site is one where you cannot navigate your way down seven different levels and not know how you ended up there or how to get back.

This is where you start looking at how your content is arranged and finding where you have clusters of content that can be restructured to provide a more intuitive flow for a visitor. This is where you start mapping out your user journeys, taking a hard look at your navigation, and really thinking about your content strategy.

There are many different tools to help with this audit. The primary ones I use are Screaming Frog, Google Analytics 4, and Hotjar or Crazy Egg for heatmaps and user monitoring.

"There is still space for your digital experts in higher ed to do good work within their role. The more informed people are, the better decisions they will make, and the better position we're in as a society. We can find ways to recruit and build our communities with intention and inclusion. That is going to serve us all well, but it's hard. ROI feels like a piddly term because there is more at stake. What we are doing here matters, and it is transformative. We have to work at thinking about outcomes at all those levels."

— Georgy Cohen, director of digital strategy, OHO Interactive

Search Audit

Now we get to the search audit, my favorite. This is where you reveal the opportunity hiding in your content. SEO is often the low-hanging fruit, especially in higher education where our .edu domain gives us an advantage over other sites by providing inherent authority.

This is when you gather information about what keywords you are already ranking for that you might not be aware of. Where are there gaps in your branded and unbranded keywords that you do not currently have content for, but should? What are the strategic keywords you should be targeting that you are not? What are your competitors and peers ranking for that you are not? What questions are users asking that you are not answering? What are your website visitors searching for on your website?

All these data points can provide a wealth of information on what content you should be creating, what content you should prioritize for optimization, and what you should be tracking.

There are a variety of SEO tools like Semrush, Moz, Ahrefs, and Majestic that can help with this process. There are also AI-powered tools like MarketMuse and BrightEdge that can provide numerous SEO insights and recommendations to help with this audit and with the optimization process.

Google does not share its algorithm with us, so we do not know exactly how it evaluates the 200+ ranking factors it uses to create its results. What they do share is their Search Engine Evaluator Guidelines.[2]

These guidelines are provided to people that Google pays to run searches and then judge the quality of the results. The feedback they provide helps Google figure out how to adjust their algorithm to provide the highest quality results possible.

This 170-page document (at the time of writing) is updated regularly. Within this document, the E-E-A-T criteria is mentioned more than 120 times. E-E-A-T stands for:

Experience: Does the creator or source of the content have firsthand or life experience with the topic?

Expertise: Do they have the necessary knowledge or skill for the topic?

Authoritativeness: Are they a go-to source for the topic?

Trust: The previous three factors, along with a few others, all go into establishing the overall trust level for the site.

We have a lot working for us as institutions, but one of the things that helps Google and evaluators identify your site as high E-E-A-T is having a breadth of content around a particular topic area. We can help showcase this by better organizing our content, using pillar pages, and connecting high-performing strategic content across our digital landscape.

When we talk about pillar pages, we are referring to high-level pages that feature a wide variety of content on a broad topic area and provide opportunities to link to other strategically important or high-traffic pages related to that topic.

Now you have all the data you need to prioritize your optimization process and identify the highest impact opportunities so you can start addressing those. Then it is time to do the actual optimization.

Optimize

At this point, I will aggregate all the data into one big sheet and begin making an Effort and Impact Matrix to help me identify the most important items that will have the largest impact. Then it is a matter of doing the optimization. Every optimization action taken should connect back to the strategic goals and focus on driving action from our users to help us meet those goals.

Every action should be measurable and tracked as a KPI on our dashboard so we can see the impact of our efforts. Then, the cycle starts again. That's right; optimization is not a one-time process. It takes constant monitoring, adjusting, and updating. Once you start ranking for keywords you were targeting, you will notice other strategic keywords start popping up that you should target. You will discover new gaps in your user journey or your content roadmap.

There are AI tools that can help with these processes. ChatGPT and other generative AI tools, like Claude, Gemini, and HyperWrite, are very good at suggesting semantically related keywords you may want to target. ChatGPT can help with data aggregation and analysis.

While the process I outlined here is focused on websites, the same model works for any type of content, social, video, and even podcasts. The amount of data you can collect and examine is more limited, but the process is the same. Think about what you want to accomplish with the content on each of your channels, what you want your users to do with that content, and how you can track it.

"A 'like' is a vote for more of that type of content. Do not forget to track how many pieces of content you put out there, because that's advertising and marketing—repeating the message."

> — Jenny Li Fowler, director of social media strategy, MIT,
> author of *Organic Social Media: How to Build Flourishing Online Communities*, host of Enrollify's *Confessions of a Higher Ed Social Media Manager* podcast

For access to templates, dashboards, and insights into other optimization processes, go to *ecmhe.com*.

EPIC THOUGHTS

- Setting up the right tracking tools (e.g., Google Analytics, Tag Manager, Search Console), KPIs, and OKRs based on strategic goals is essential before collecting data. Custom events, tags, and data layer variables may be needed for granular tracking.

- A comprehensive website optimization process includes strategic, user, analytics, technical performance, information architecture, and search audits. Insights from each inform content opportunities, user journey improvements, and keyword targets.

- Benchmarking current content performance, setting up dashboards to monitor ongoing KPIs, and prioritizing optimizations based on projected impact are key. Optimization should always tie back to strategic goals and driving user actions.

- SEO presents significant opportunity for higher education given the authority of .edu domains. Focusing content around topics where the institution has high E-E-A-T (Experience, Expertise, Authoritativeness, Trust) and using pillar pages can boost search performance.

- Optimization is a continuous process of monitoring, adjusting, and updating based on new data insights, not a one-time event. AI tools can help with keyword research, data analysis, and content suggestions to aid the process, but human expertise is still needed.

EPIC RESOURCES

1.   V. F. Ridgway, "Dysfunctional Consequences of Performance Measurements," *Administrative Science Quarterly* 1, no. 2 (September 1956), https://doi.org/10.2307/2390989 (archived at https://perma.cc/2TQS-URCK), 240.

2.   "Search Quality Evaluator Guidelines," Google, last update March 5, 2024, https://static.googleusercontent.com/media/guidelines.raterhub.com/en//searchqualityevaluator guidelines.pdf.

CHAPTER 14

Community

One of the biggest opportunities I see for connecting with our audiences in higher education is the use of community. I see very few institutions leveraging these platforms as a way to get our audiences to know, like, and trust us. In many cases, all we need to do is show up and try to help.

As our audiences have less faith and trust in the information they find through search engines, social search, or AI-search, they will look for communities where they can connect with real human experts or other people like themselves.

"Community building from the very beginning, from a prospective student through becoming an alumnus, is where you can build that lifelong individual committed to being a part of that community. We need to invest in creative ways to make them feel valued. If we can get to that, schools will win those audiences."

— Harrison "Soup" Campbell, head of community experience, ZeeMee

Among his many accolades, Mark Schaefer is the author of *Belonging to the Brand*, a deep dive into the value and potential of community for businesses. It also applies to higher education, possibly even more so than businesses.

A typical student, faculty, or staff member spends several years at an institution. Much of that time is spent on campus. The majority of their interactions are with other students, faculty, or staff. Then the students often become alumni.

Throughout that entire process, we have so many opportunities to bring those people into various communities where they can make connections that might last their entire lives. We have some of this through our clubs and organizations, but there are additional avenues we could use to connect current students with potential students, alumni, or employers. We could connect graduate students with other researchers or alumni working in their fields.

"Once people subscribe to your content in a virtual way, they are opting into you. They are saying, 'I believe in you. I love what you are doing. I want to learn more. It's okay for you to market to me.' Unfortunately, that is where most universities stop. They do not go to that extra level, which is community, the ultimate emotional connection. Not only do people connect to the brand, they also connect to each other. And the research suggests that bond is even stronger. The strategy in a community is not building the connection to the brand, it's building the connection to each other. Because if you get people to become friends, collaborate, co-create, and work together on things in a community, they are never going to leave you, they are never going to leave that community; they literally belong to the brand. That is just such an overlooked strategy. It could be the biggest idea for universities because there is so much emotion and passion inherently built into the brand."

> — Mark Schaefer, executive director, Schaefer Marketing Solutions,
> speaker, author, host of *The Marketing Companion* podcast

New first-year students face an incredible range of emotions, from anxiety to excitement, freedom to homesickness, loneliness to self-discovery. Leaving home and moving onto a college campus can be terrifying. Providing those new students with connections on campus could have a huge impact on retention, success, and mental health.

"Connected students thrive, point blank. The more connections they have, the greater the chance they will thrive. If these incoming students can make those tight-knit, close connections, friendship groups, and relationships with key stakeholders at the college or university, they hit the ground running as soon as they get on campus. That is why community is so important. That is why it should start months before they have even applied to that school, so you extend the time for those relationships to deepen and strengthen. That sets students up to have the greatest success as they transition from high school to college."

— Harrison "Soup" Campbell, head of community experience, ZeeMee

While creating community environments could have a huge impact, they take constant management and active engagement. Especially at the beginning. There needs to be value to the user for spending their time in the community, and there needs to be timely feedback.

"The belonging piece is such a core for all humans. Students want to feel like they belong, whether that is to Greek life or whether that's in the residence hall. And it is so easy to throw up a Discord or a Facebook group. But no matter the industry or audience, those take a ton of work. I don't know if higher ed is ready for that kind of resource."

— Josie Ahlquist, Dr. Josie Ahlquist, Inc.,
digital engagement and leadership consultant

Many community platforms exist, but you are back in a situation of building on rented land. These platforms are also constantly improving and updating functionality, so someone needs to be able to spend time adjusting the strategy and making sure users are aware of changes that might impact them.

"One of the challenges with communities is where that community exists. It's worth trying to find a way to build a community where it can be an owned space, but that is hard. There will be risks, but that should not make you shy away from it. You need sharp individuals who can adapt, be flexible, and grow with the platform as it evolves and changes. That's the biggest challenge."

— Harrison "Soup" Campbell, head of community experience, ZeeMee

The next few years will see a huge growth in community opportunities and platforms. More schools are starting to recognize the value of creating these connections and environments that can extend beyond the life cycle of a student's time on campus.

The evolution of AR and VR technology is going to exponentially expand community opportunities that will extend beyond our institutions and into the global landscape. The sooner we can start recognizing and preparing for these changes, the sooner we will be ready to take advantage of them.

"The biggest issue is relevance. If you create a community that is relevant to your students, to your alumni, then they are going to help you be relevant as a university."

> — Mark Schaefer, executive director, Schaefer Marketing Solutions, speaker, author, host of *The Marketing Companion* podcast

As said in Chapter 9, "How to Create Epic Content Marketing," you need to think about the messenger. Who will be the most trusted voice for the audience you are trying to connect with? How can you build a community of those voices to talk to new members of that audience?

"Everyone in higher ed knows the value of leveraging your current students for that authentic, peer-to-peer connection. However, the holy grail is not current students but other prospective students themselves. That is what very few colleges and universities have yet to discover or tap into. It's through community, relationships, and connections that students influence each other. On ZeeMee, prospective students can influence each other in that way. They are applying at 3.5x, yielding at 4x, and melt is cut in half because of those connections, those relationships, and influencing each other."

> — Harrison "Soup" Campbell, head of community experience, ZeeMee

Communities can also create lifetime networks and connect people who would have never met otherwise but who share common interests and passions. One of the biggest reasons that students come to college is to get a better job. Connecting with alumni who are already working in fields the students are interested in is the best way to find out if that career is what they expected and to create opportunities to find internships that may lead to full-time jobs.

"Community is everything, and we need to niche down. Finding the MIT students in your hometown, or in your home state, and having them talk to students that are interested in coming to MIT because they know the environment they're from, they know the perceptions of MIT, and in a different state, that might be different than Massachusetts. Niche down. Have it smaller, more intimate, and person to person."

> — Jenny Li Fowler, director of social media strategy, MIT,
> author of *Organic Social Media: How to Build Flourishing Online Communities*, host of Enrollify's *Confessions of a Higher Ed Social Media Manager* podcast

Leveraging community is the future of brands, including higher education. As customers get more protective of their data, as regulations make purchased lists more difficult to obtain, and as consumers become even more aware of when they are being marketed to, positioning ourselves as helpful expert voices in these communities of trust will become a primary means of connection.

"You do not need to convince me that community is a good thing. I think the challenge for schools is how they create that. How do they build these things? Because to get someone to go to a space regularly, and connect with people, and love being there, in a brand space, my word . . . we struggle to get people there now when we do lead gen magnets for them. How are we going to get them to go and enjoy themselves with us? It's a complete mind shift in how we think about marketing and measure it."

> — Kyle Campbell, founder and managing director, Education Marketer

EPIC THOUGHTS

- Building communities where audiences can connect with experts and each other is a huge opportunity for higher education, as people seek trusted information outside of search engines and AI.

- Students who feel a sense of belonging and form connections through communities are more likely to thrive. Engaging prospective students in communities months before they enroll can increase application and yield rates while reducing melt.

- Successful communities require significant ongoing management, engagement, and resources to provide value to members and timely feedback. Institutions must be prepared for this level of commitment and have adaptable staff to manage evolving platforms.

- Peer-to-peer connections, like prospective students influencing each other or current students and alumni sharing authentic experiences, are the "holy grail" of higher education marketing. Communities are the ideal environment to foster these relationships.

- As data privacy regulations tighten and consumers become more marketing-savvy, building trusted communities will be essential for institutions to connect with audiences long-term. It requires a complete mindset shift in how higher education approaches marketing and measurement.

CHAPTER 15

Predictions

One of my favorite parts of writing this book was getting to ask experts their thoughts on the future of higher education and what it would look like in five years. Answers and predictions were all over the board. After I asked the question, I qualified it by saying they could tell me what they legitimately thought it was going to be, or what they hoped it would be.

"I think there is going to be an explosion of content. There's going to be so much noise and volume. But there are also going to be people that crave authenticity and small scale. There is going to be a need for authentic, curated, small-scale, personalized content, even more than we have now. We are going to have less tolerance for the generic because we are going to know that the generic didn't come from a person. Schools without a brand will struggle. If you don't have a strong way to differentiate yourself and be distinct in the market, you are going to disappear. You are going to be buried in the volume and the noise.

This is the time for you to invest in a robust differentiation strategy for your brand, brought alive through content and experiences. When people see something with your unique vibe, they are going to know it's you. You can't come up with this five years from now, you have to do it now."

— Dayana Kibilds, strategist, Ologie, speaker, co-author of *Mailed It: A Guide to Crafting Emails That Build Relationships and Get Results*, host of Enrollify's *Talking Tactics* podcast

"Universities are getting to a place where there is going to be some desperation for a lot of schools --they are going to have to get outside their comfort zone. I think in the next five years, we will see some big winners for universities that dip their toe into content creation in different ways than before. I think the majority will stick to what they know, and they are going to miss out on some big opportunities. If we keep doing what we have always done, a lot of schools are going to shut down. There has to be a level of adapting and pivoting. Looking outside of higher ed is going to be where the answers are."

— Rob Clark, director of strategic engagement, Greenville University

"Higher ed is exploding into this portfolio of options. I think what you will have is fewer, stronger organizations and fewer, stronger brands. Some will be institutions, some will be companies that the education consumer can choose from. The ones that were created because the demographics could support it 100 years ago will not be here because we don't need that anymore."

— Bill Faust, president, Ologie

"I think there is going to be a much tighter integration between marketing, communications, and IT teams because the marketing technology component of it is so critical. The martech stack is going to determine how successful universities can be in this work in a lot of ways. If you do not get that tech stack right, if you do not have the right integrations and the right connections on the back end, doing some of this work can become really difficult."

— Angela Polec, vice president for strategic marketing and communications, Temple University

"I am hopeful that marketing and comms leaders will have more of a spot at the leadership table for those bigger conversations outside of just promotion. There is going to be a lot more AI presence in our work."

> — Carrie Phillips, chief communications and marketing officer,
> University of Arkansas at Little Rock

"In five years, higher education is going to look almost identical to what it looks like today. There will be some marginal change, but higher education operates on a much longer time horizon than business. There is something to be said for stability. It also points to the incredible resilience and endurance of these models. Every year the pundits say: this is it, higher education as we know it is dead. And guess what? You are still going to college for four years. Where the changes are going to take place will be in the ways in which those institutions can be smart about extending their brand and intellectual assets in new places. But I do not think the campus experience is going to change much. From a business standpoint, it would make perfect sense for smaller schools to consolidate operations and curriculum."

> — Michael Schoenfeld, partner, global co-lead for foundations,
> education, and global health sector, Brunswick Group

"Until faculty and staff understand that social media is the CV now, there is going to be this belief that, 'I am a tenured professor, why would I spend time making videos on TikTok, or Instagram, or even LinkedIn?' There has got to be a reputational change about those activities that has to happen campus-wide. Publish or perish has been around for 80 years. Why can't 'publish' also include social media?"

> — Jay Baer, business growth and customer experience researcher,
> author, advisor, speaker

"In the future, university education is going to have to look a lot more like the competitors that are out there right now. What are the competitors? Alternative learning platforms like Amazon and Google, where you can take classes for $49 and when you finish these classes, you can have a job."

> — Mark Schaefer, executive director, Schaefer Marketing Solutions,
> speaker, author, host of *The Marketing Companion* podcast

"More schools will close. More of those will be HBCUs, unfortunately. There will be a demand for variety in its delivery. And [higher education] will be even more politicized."

— Kevin Tyler, senior vice president and practice lead,
Collaborative Communications Group

"Higher education has always been a reflection of our country. We are a closer map to how well society is functioning, or how dysfunctional it is, than other industries. For that reason, I think our campuses will be reflective of the further disconnect underway in society, the deepening of the haves and the have-nots, and the perception of us versus them. The fascinating part is that we like to talk about higher education as a service to all, but it can only be a service to all and a benefit to society if we come together in some critical ways. I don't know that we will be there in five years, or even ten. In a lot of ways, higher education is the canary in the coal mine, but we do not move quickly enough to save ourselves from the worsening conditions of the coal mine even as we gasp for breath."

— Teresa Valerio Parrot, EdD, APR, principal, TVP Communications,
co-host of *Trusted Voices* podcast

"A lot of schools are going to be closed. It's all four-year cycles. If you have a significant drop in the first year, you are not going to recover in four or five years unless you do drastic things. You are going to see a lot more mergers, and many schools are going to work with combined marketing departments or skeleton staff. Leadership is going to be a challenge.

There will still be people who need education. There is going to be a lot more diversity in our freshman incoming classes, from an undergrad perspective, and there is going to be a lot more reliance on graduate and adult learning to pay the bills. Marketing departments are going to do a whole lot more with less, which is great news for small schools that don't have any marketing department to begin with; they have got one or two people. They are going to have people who are creating an orchestra with AI and able to do things they could never have imagined. They are going to be smart and scrappy and be able to do it well. Then you are going to have the big schools that have 350 people on staff looking around saying, 'Do we really need to have 350 people on staff?' There is going to be a reckoning."

— Bart Caylor, president and founder, Caylor Solutions,
president, The Higher Ed Marketer, author of *Chasing Mission Fit*

"Emphasizing career readiness will become increasingly important to prospective students as the student body's demographics drastically change over the next five years. This rings especially true for nontraditional or first-generation students, who focus on flexibility, affordability, and a pragmatic postsecondary experience. Higher ed marketing departments must communicate what these 'new traditional' students want and remember that these students do not care about your product or service. They care about themselves, their wants, and their needs."

— Chris Rapozo, marketing specialist, Hannon Hill,
host of *Marketing Tales* podcast

"Higher education as an industry will continue to adapt to consumer behavior, competition, internal pressure to meet revenue goals, and perceptions from society. The impact of that might mean more college closures, unfortunately, or continued shifts in how education is delivered. It might also mean increasingly leaner budgets for marcom to do more with.

One area that worries me in the present and the future is the attacks from certain segments of society on diversity, equity, and inclusion initiatives in colleges and universities. The recent ruling from the US Supreme Court on the use of affirmative action in admissions is just a precursor of what is to come. As a Black man in America, it is sickening to watch institutions undo some of the progress we have made simply for fear of backlash from bad-faith actors.

On a positive note, we have seen a shift in marcom staffing strategies. Instead of relying on internal staff and hiring people (which is financially challenging), teams have hired less staff while partnering with agencies to fill expertise gaps and help strategically reach their goals. At the same time, SimpsonScarborough published research in

2022 that showed experienced marcom professionals were leaving their institutions to work on the agency side. I am interested in seeing the future of marcom teams in both institutions and agencies as we continue working together to advance higher education."

— Joshua Charles, director of web strategy and technology,
Rutgers Business School

"The higher ed marketing function has come a long way in the last 30 years. The higher ed CMO has arrived and is making a big difference on college campuses. But colleges and universities are still behind other industries in terms of developing integrated, strategic, powerful, measurable marcom programs. Most institutions are still investing only a teeny tiny portion of their operating budget in marketing and there is a severe lack of coordination of the marketing and communications effort across most campuses, especially those that are mid to large. At most large universities, each college or school has its own marketing department that operates largely independently from the central marketing department. They duplicate efforts, compete for adwords, and miss opportunities to build a unified brand for their institution. I am excited about the fact that this will likely improve in the next five to ten years. The marketing effort will become even more integrated, even more sophisticated, even more focused on measurable results than ever. My biggest worry? It won't happen fast enough."

— Elizabeth Scarborough Johnson, chairman, SimpsonScarborough

"The higher ed institutions that will still be around will be those that grasp that the pandemic forever changed what people want. Students who had no interest in any form of online learning because they wanted the full college experience [have]now gotten used to learning online, and it is not scary or intimidating, or seen as inferior. The institutions that grab that hybrid model by the horns will be the most successful. Those that ask the questions that lead to a better product will be successful. In terms of higher ed marketing and what it will look like, I think we are going to be aided a lot more by AI. I think AI is going to help us make better decisions about our audiences, how to reach them, where to reach them, and what message will reach them. If marketers are not spending the time to understand and learn these tools, I think they are going to be in big trouble in their careers over the next few years."

— Jaime Hunt, chief marketing officer, Old Dominion University,
host of *Confessions of a Higher Ed CMO* podcast

"As preferences for modality and the need for skills-based learning become more prevalent, higher education will need to adapt rapidly over the next five years. We can no longer focus on changing our marketing message and hope it resonates. The 'product' of higher education must transform to meet the evolving needs of today's learners and tomorrow's leaders."

— Gil Rogers, higher education and student evangelist

"More schools will embrace remote work and distributed teams so they can attract higher quality applicants who may not live down the street from the school. The integration of AI will be ubiquitous, and every school will have a chatbot."

— Mallory Willsea, VP marketing, Element451,
chief strategist, Enrollify, host of *Higher Ed Pulse* podcast

"For the institutions that thrive, there will be more efficiency created, volume served, and growth for those teams. Teams will have to leverage the tools that allow you to do this work efficiently. I think these teams can demonstrate ROI and secure the FTEs need and the budgets they need. Cabinet leadership is becoming a lot more aware of what marketing can do for institutions."

— Ashley Budd, senior marketing director, Cornell University,
co-author of *Mailed It: A Guide to Crafting Emails That Build
Relationships and Get Results*

"Universities that provide diverse experiences to their students are going to be considered more valuable than ever. The places that show value beyond just sitting at your computer and getting a credential are going to be even more valuable, and we need to market that value to prospective students. There is going to be value in place and community that we, as marketers, are going to have to sell."

> — Dave Tyler, director of university social media,
> Rochester Institute of Technology

"Unfortunately, I think we will see more of the same. Higher ed is, collectively, notoriously stubborn. Just a few years ago, we were referencing 'at least 4,000 colleges and universities.' Now, we are referencing 'fewer than . . . .' Until a lot of major problems make life difficult for the biggest names, higher ed will keep moving along as if everything is all right. That said, I am really worried that higher ed will remain 10 years behind the private sector in sound business practices, which includes marketing and communications. What excites me, however, is Generation Z. So far, they have a reputation for demanding authentic leadership. I think they are going to be loud about demanding that higher ed does a better job."

> — Eddie Francis, brand strategy consultant/principal,
> Edify Ventures, LLC, host of *I Wanna Work There!* podcast

"We will have more of a collaborative space and partners. We will see a shift in the perceptions of what it means to be a modern-day professor. We are seeing this right now. We are being evaluated on more than just teaching and research. We are looking at, 'Where are you speaking? Are you doing interesting partnerships? How are you doing in terms of engaged learning and community activities?'"

> — Karen Freberg, professor of strategic communication,
> University of Louisville, director, The Bird's Nest Student Agency

"I think we are going to see a continued shift toward AI-generated content, not only text based, but video based, to the point where what is AI-generated and what is human generated will be indistinguishable. In a lot of ways I think this is really cool, because, once again, it's a lowering of the barrier to entry into getting our message heard by a global audience. You no longer have to be a seasoned writer or have access to a video studio and technicians that know how to operate that equipment in order to produce content in those ways. This excites me because it opens us all up to new ways of creating that we may not have explored otherwise.

At the same time, it's scary because the line between what is real and fake is being blurred. So building trust over time with our audiences, as well as building community, will be more important than ever, as opposed to 'random acts of content.' I also think that it will be important to both embrace these new technologies [while] at the same time lean into our ability as humans to experience empathy. If we can find ways to truly listen to and understand the emotions of our audiences, and all the internal and external factors affecting their thoughts around college, we will have a better chance at influencing them in unique ways."

> — John Azoni, owner and executive producer, Unveild,
> host of *Higher Ed Storytelling University* podcast

"In five years, there will be a deeper integration with marketing across other aspects of institutional operations. Curriculum should be imbued with some sensibilities for marketing. Content marketing is not just posts and articles. It is also events and activities, experiences, touchpoints. It is word of mouth. It is all the things that are influenced by those outputs. There is a real need to have deeper integration in order for it to feel authentic and real. If you take that same principle of deeply understanding your audience's needs, challenges, interests, barriers, and all of that, then you are solving for your audience too. Content marketing becomes a component of a broader effort to rethink how we offer higher education to our students and make it more relevant and remain resonant and meaningful.

There will be a drowning out of schools that do not invest in brand, whether that is [by] financially drowning out or just visibility and interests. The critical challenge for marketers in the next five years is: how do we not suffer that fate? What do we do to ensure that we are providing value, number one, and communicating value, number two? Communicating value should come after providing it."

> — Tim Jones, director, brand and integrated strategy,
> SimpsonScarborough

"My vision of higher ed in five years is: you log in on your Vision Pro, you take whatever class you want from wherever you want. The walls are broken down. Applying to a school becomes more about what resources they have for my mental health, for my career development, for professional development. You can take classes from any campus. It's not that you go to a room, it's that you go to the well, and you pull the information that you want out. And you drink that information in a way that feeds you and fuels you. Then you get certified.

We come up with this framework of how you still get a diploma or some sort of recognition, or maybe it's something else -- but it is learning what you want, from who you want, where you want. That is what I would love to see from higher ed in five years."

— Andrew Cassel, director of communications and science engagement, Hubbard Brook Research Foundation

"One of my biggest concerns for the future is that nothing changes, and we keep pumping out three-year and four-year programs. That we ignore all the signs that students want shorter courses and better digital experiences. That is what we need to be looking at. Eventually, your audience, who have grown up on Roblox and are used to having a really good online experience, get to higher ed, and they go, 'What is this?' And they look for alternatives.

Higher ed marketing will be content-led. I do not see how it can't be. At the moment we are creating spamming campaigns. We are simply renting the same audience every year when we should be building something. I think future universities will be much more focused on what they want to stand for. They will look at their course content and how they can repurpose that for an audience to start educating them earlier in the journey."

— Kyle Campbell, founder and managing director, Education Marketer

"We are going to continue to see more mergers and acquisitions of schools. A lot of schools are starting to think about what the new model of education looks like. We are all responding to the lack of confidence we're seeing across the country. Financial challenges are making institutions struggle more. We are going to see more niche institutions pop up. Universities are starting to realize they can't be all things to all people because they can't afford it anymore. They have to hone in on what they are good at, and let go of some of the things they're not. We are going see a huge shift in more institutions starting to cut the programs that do not work for them. The death of the humanities is not going to happen, because there are institutions that excel at that. It just means that not everybody is going to have all the humanities programs."

— Jamie Ceman, senior executive vice president, RW Jones Agency

"Communication will have to be more personal, human, and social. We genuinely need to help our candidates in the process. We do a disservice to our results if students can't find what they want to study and where they will be. Content marketing teams will be truly student-centric and focused on understanding every detail of what our students go through, what they need, and when. You would think that is where we would be already, but a content revolution is slowly happening, and the future is bright."

— Emanuel Díaz, head of content marketing, IE University

"We [community colleges] are positioned well for what is to come because we do a lot of short-term career training. We offer trades and skilled labor programs that most four-year institutions don't, and that is a huge gap in the workplace. We need to reevaluate what types of skills and education people need going forward. In general, people do not want associate degrees in general education. They want something where they can learn the skill, apply it right away, get a job, and do it as quickly as possible. Education will continue to be important, but how we deliver it and what we teach will change. I don't know how, but it has to change."

— Maya Demishkevich, chief marketing officer,
Carroll Community College

"Over the next five years we will continue to experience declines in demand driven by a combination of population dynamics (e.g., the demographic cliff) as well as softening consumer confidence in the value of a degree and declines in degree requirements from employers.

Combining all of that with an increasingly noisy world means it will be harder than ever to get noticed, drive engagement, and meaningfully spark interest and drive action among our primary target audiences."

— Seth Odell, founder and CEO, Kanahoma,
co-host of *Higher Ed Pulse* podcast

"We are going to go through a period of really having to make sure that the impact, value, and benefit of not only higher education but higher education research is valued and understood, and that we understand the challenges that are facing us as an industry and as an institution. I think that there is a chasm between so-called select universities and other universities; some universities are not thinking about, or worried about, enrollment, and many other institutions are feeling that pain in great detail. It is incumbent upon every one of us to not think only about our institutions, but to think about what benefit we ae providing to our country and our world. To think about that and help people understand, and be reminded, and to genuinely look at some of the things that are troubling about higher ed, and then say, 'Is that a misunderstanding, or is that something we have to think about evolving?' Because I think we are in for a pretty rough road."

— Paul Rand, vice president of communications, University of Chicago,
host of *Big Brains* podcast

"In five years, broadly speaking, we are going to look reasonably similar, but I think we will be starting to chase our tails quite a lot. I think we will be in a position where, if we have not changed something, we will be starting to get very scared. We will start to see the shifts in ten years. We will not see programs looking the way they look at the moment. We will see a radical overhaul of what a product is in the higher education space and a reinvention of that. My hope is that we will see a much more fluid approach for people to be able to study this module from this university and that module from that university. This is where I think the globalization piece offers such an opportunity. From an international perspective, we will see a broader distribution, rather than just UK and US universities. AI will also be a big driver of that, particularly when it comes to things like translation. But I think we are going to see our sector cling on for as long as it possibly can to not change."

— Tracy Playle, chief content strategist, Pickle Jar Communications,
author of *The Connected Campus*

We are at the beginning of a new era in higher education, where the power of content marketing, storytelling, and technology will drive the survival and success of institutions, especially smaller ones.

Covid-19 taught us that higher education can adapt, which is what we are going to need to do (a lot) in the next five years. We are facing so many disruptions. The impact that AI is going to have on knowledge transfer and education will be transformative. The impact it will have on marketing and content discoverability will require us to think in new ways and pay attention to what brands are doing to adapt.

Once augmented reality and virtual reality devices become more widely adopted as the form factors are reduced, the entire dynamic of content consumption and learning will be altered.

Our lives will become more global as virtual environments create opportunities to collaborate and learn across distances, without language barriers. Communities will spring up around different areas of interest and research to create integrated and diverse learning opportunities and cultural exposure to new ideas and viewpoints.

I am optimistic that we will find ways to make learning more democratized so we can provide our expertise to a global audience regardless of their resources and funding.

There will still be students who will want the full on-campus experience, but their classes may be taught by faculty from around the world and held in interactive virtual environments. For many areas of specialization, they will still need access to sensitive and expensive equipment for research and training.

We will need to partner more with businesses to create real-world experience opportunities for our students. I think this will be one of the biggest leverage points for institutions to help students get better jobs and to help businesses find the skilled talent they need.

We will create communities with our students, faculty, staff, and alumni that will establish a lifelong sense of connection and purpose. We will work across institutions and across borders to solve our most pressing problems.

Education is all about finding ways to teach people how to transform our world into a better place. We have the opportunity to do that if we agree on our strategy, connect with the right audiences, share the right information and knowledge, and keep track of our progress to stay focused on our goals.

It's just like content marketing.

Index